MW00377672

Introduction

A few years ago I was just an average guy, going thru life with little thought to the concept of changing my life. I was caught up in the simple struggle to survive and get by. Through a series of events that were sort of hard to explain, I met a teacher who started me on a fascinating journey of self discovery.

I went into this with no thought of the end game, but instead just went along because energy healing was something the wife and I were both interested in and the opportunity was there. It wasn't long before I realized that this was real and I was not just playing with my imagination. That changed everything.

Real changes started happening to me. Changes in my body, changes in my mindset, and changes in my entire way of looking at life started to manifest. I realized that my reflexes improved, and I lost a hundred pounds. I began to feel a confidence that I never thought I would have in my life.

The way people perceived me changed also and I found myself in a much different position than I thought I was in. The power of focusing your mind is real and tangible and it soon shows in real results with just a little practice.

I was searching for something more in this life. These techniques changed my life for the better and let me find out who I really am as opposed to who I have been told I am. The process has been fascinating to undergo, and with all the changes already under my belt I can't wait to see what tomorrow brings and who I will be then.

So, Dear readers, it is my hope that all of you can become more than you are now, and in the process, help everyone around you to also be happier. This can be a better world if we can change the way we look at it. The small efforts this practice takes are well worth the effort and I sincerely want others to be able to enjoy feeling like I do.

Table of Contents:

The Philosophy of Two Dogs

I was a young guy in middle school science class when I first got introduced to the concept of atoms, molecules, and light. My mind started working on the concepts that formed the base of my belief systems today.

I realized that all we see is an electro-photochemical reaction that occurs in the mysterious organ we call the brain. Our eyes, ears, and skin somehow converted these reflecting light rays into what we came to believe to be our reality. I never saw my world quite the same again.

I realized my memories and experiences had somehow been converted to electrical impulses that could be recalled at will, and a staggering number of them were available at my slightest whim. This was an amazing concept to me, and greatly enhanced my perceptions, and started me thinking about consciousness.

When I was 17 I hooked up with a spiritual little girl who opened my eyes to the spirits, and I was suddenly faced with the fact of an afterlife, and I was forced to alter my belief systems. Once you see things move seemingly by themselves you are changed forever.

You have to believe, or else I think you would go insane. I mean really, it is one or the other isn't it? Either that vase just jumped off the shelf and flew past your wife's head on its own, or else you are out of your mind, which one is it?

If it happens once you may doubt yourself, and find a way to justify it in your mind. Your brain will try to compensate for what it feels is something that does not fit into its idea of "reality." But, if it happens over and then over again, you are faced with another choice and you have to face a new version of "reality".

So as a kid, my brain was enthusiastic about anything of the paranormal variety, and I read every book in the local library about any subject I could find, from ghosts, to religions, to psychology, to science and physics textbooks.

I soaked up everything I could find and understand on quantum theory, quantum mechanics, and string theory. Even though it was too much for my young mind to absorb, I retained enough to keep me thinking and making connections. I was always seeking and evolving my belief system. You have to in order to grow. When you stop seeking you stop moving forward.

As everyone does, though, I grew up and got started with my life. I married that witchy little girl, moved out West, and had kids. I was off the path for a good number of years, and was just living from day to day. I was living just to exist and stumbling through my day to day struggles with no spiritual influence in my life.

I was going around and around circling that proverbial mountain and afraid to climb it. I was going through life thinking like I was a spiritual person, but identifying with nothing really.

Life was quickly going no place, working all the time just to pay for it all, and I came to a place where a lot of people get to in their lives and I was depressed. I tried this and that medication, and just about lost my mind trying to find happiness in a little pill. I didn't know it but I was about to have my first spiritual awakening.

One day I was seriously contemplating suicide, and in real desperation for the first time in my life, I found myself in my weakness turning to a God I never really believed in for a path. I made the first earnest and humble prayer I had ever made in my life, and asked God to simply give me a path, and show me a way to live in this world.

He took me by the shoulders and made me look at someone I had never really paid much attention to. An old guy I always liked but never really bothered to make friends with. You know how it is in a big business place. Turns out he is a minister. Things started happening quickly from there.

A remarkable series of coincidences happened that were such as to be undeniable, and I found myself in a very fundamentalist Southern Baptist church. I tried very hard to listen to their message, and take it to heart. I had some very positive and spiritual moments in that church.

However, they turned on us when we told them we had ghosts, and told us we were communing with familiar spirits, and that this was unacceptable. Then they found out we had gay friends, and insisted we try to influence them to come to the church so the elders could "talk" to them. We refused, and that drew the line in the sand.

After that, they had a special breakfast with us and the elders told us that 10% of my gross income was a prerequisite to membership in their church, and that I should kindly make that directly payable from my bank account by automatic withdrawal on a bi-weekly payment schedule. They even had the paperwork for me to fill out. I knew that if I had to pay for the word, I was not in the right place.

I declined, and my search for guidance continued. The spirits continued to make themselves known in our lives, and kept me thinking about the supernatural, or the natural as I believed it to be. I had the nagging urge to do energy work with my aura. I knew I could somehow manipulate my aura to enhance healing and help ease pain. I was yet to discover the river of energy that flows through us all.

Our First Real Energy Experience

One night I asked my wife to do some visualization with me. I wanted to work with our auras, and combine our auras, and each visualize what they looked like, and what our experience was, and then later to write it down and compare notes, before we discussed it.

We were sitting in a dark room, legs crossed facing one another, my palms out and down, and her palms up and touching mine. We both started our silent visualization. I saw our auras combining and flowing around each other like lovers. I decided to totally encompass her aura with my own, and seal her in my energy like a warm hug.

I began to visualize this happening, and suddenly I made some sort of connection. I saw a white-silver string with a glowing drop of energy at the end of it shoot out of the top of our aura and shoot up into the sky, and it suddenly just disappeared into a huge green ocean of the same energy with a beautiful ripple, and I was suddenly connected for the first time to the "ALL."

It was like a download of information that left me reeling. I suddenly pulled back into myself and broke the connection, coming back into my body like when you wake up suddenly from a falling dream, startling myself back to reality.

Our hands pulled apart, and my wife said, "Do you see that?" I looked around and what I had at first thought to be the visual purple effect of night vision, I saw instead was a pale blue glow of cool flames dancing around the floor all around the bed, like St. Elmo's fire.

Suddenly I had the impression that we were playing dangerous games, and that we should do some research before we ever attempted to do anything like that again. Years went by with us never again attempting anything like that, and me never doing anything more than using my hands as electrodes and using my own energy to move it through my wife and ease her pains.

Our point by point comparison of the experience we had was amazingly similar. Both of us envisioned the same "all"

This was a powerful experience for us and gave us a lot to think about.

Ghost Hunting

At some point we got a digital camera, and made a playful attempt to do some ghost hunting. We got some incredible pictures our first time out. We were in an old Pioneer cemetery, very old tombstones. We got pictures with faces in them and full body spirits, and other anomalous things.

We quickly got bored with ghost hunting, after gathering many cool pictures and even a few evp's. My impression fit with the Native way of thinking we had come to adopt, that there are spirits all around us all the time. I think we literally wade through them everywhere we go as our ancestors watch over us.

The South American Shamans are appalled by the Western and European people. They say we do not know how to send on our dead, as they say there are hordes of ancestors travelling with each one they see.

In some of their belief systems, it is necessary to gently separate the chakras from the physical remains at the time of death, and then push the soul free by gently pushing on the sole of the feet.

Our energy and consciousness goes on, back to the all taking with it all that we have learned. Science has shown us that energy cannot be destroyed, it simply changes form. Our consciousness is pure energy, and since we know that energy cannot be destroyed, we know that it goes on in some form. This is evident in spirit activity.

I think some people are simply vibrating at a frequency that makes them better receptors for the spirits to be able to communicate. I think the spirits are the same vital energy that makes up our consciousness, and that energy can never die, so it simply changes from one form to another, corporeal to incorporeal. Some people just sense it better than others. It is still cognizant and aware.

Eventually I came to realize through various chains of events that these same spirits were guiding us by the nose, and taking our lives in a definite direction. We came to live in a place that was very spiritually significant to us, unbeknownst to us at the time we bought the place. Not on the most positive level, but obviously to do with the spirits in our life.

I at some point made a conscious decision to quit second guessing myself and go with my first instinctive impulse, and let the spirits guide me. It has led to some incredible things happening in my life.

I have come to humbly be included with an incredibly diverse circle of healers and shamans and medicine people, teachers and students all. I still can't believe that I am a part of this beautiful circle, and yet somehow I know things are going exactly as they should, and that the creator is making it all happen just like it is supposed to be happening.

I am supposed to be learning these things. I am supposed to be using the energy around us, and showing others how to do it too. I am supposed to be bathing the world in healing light and love, countering the pain and the horrors of some other's experience like a white light blood cell. They may be my horrors someday, so doing what I can now to stop it is in my own best interest as well as yours. You would not be reading this if you did not want to make the world a better place.

Meditation

These great people taught me to meditate. Meditation is the core of my practice now, and I find that it is necessary to practice meditation in order to learn to focus your mind and keep it focused. Keeping your mind focused is key to any kind of visionary work. You have to be able to visualize, and keep that visualization and focus to move the energy and apply it in healing.

Before this talk is finished I will have delved into various meditation techniques, South American Shamanism, Polynesian Huna, where we will talk about the Higher and Lower selves, not to be confused with the Christian idea of familiar spirits. These are instead two parts of your own beautiful spirit, and it was given to you by the Creator to learn to know and love.

I will talk about some Native American Shamanism, and how to discover your totem animals and vision quest. I will talk about qi' gong and Chi kung, and how to gather energy from the earth and sky and apply it through visualization and mental focus to various healing techniques.

Energy

First, I'd like to talk a little bit about Energy. We are truly creatures of energy. The actual physical matter that makes up what we know as ourselves is composed of very little mass. If all the empty space were to be removed from our bodies, we would fit many times over on the head of a pin.

Were you to knock on something near you, you may think that it is solid enough. It feels hard, it stops our hand. It reflects light. In reality there is very little difference between that and the air next to it. What makes that object solid is simply energy bonding on a molecular level.

 Our energy and its energy are not vibrating at the same frequency, so our particles do not interact. If we knock hard enough it creates more energy... pain.

We are a beautiful conscious energy that was given the divine ability to love and grow and evolve. We do this through good and evil alike, and we are supposed to learn from the evil in the world, and not perpetuate it as society seems to be doing today.

Our consciousness is also energy. Our consciousness is much more than the gray matter contained inside our skulls. We receive all sorts of information from outside of our heads. Ever hear of mother's intuition? ESP?

Psychic ability is natural to us. Like the birds "know" where to migrate, and the salmon unerringly swim back up stream to their birthplace, we human beings just "know" things.

Mothers somehow know if their child is in pain. My wife knew one time when I was in a car accident. She has demonstrated this many times in our marriage, and before we met back to her childhood.

Where does that information come from? It definitely does not come from within our brains. Our brain is a receptor. It tunes in on the energy that connects all of us. I put forth to you that there really is a collective consciousness that stores the experiences of all living things, and that we can tap into this collective consciousness for information we have no way of knowing in the physically limited world we live in.

We are taught from the time we are first aware that there is a fantasy world, and a "real" world. In many cultures that line is very vague and indistinct. Only in our plastic and deep fried western culture is it scoffed at. Much of the world takes it as a matter of course.

In South America and other places, shamans ingest a mixture of plants that produces intense hallucinations. They go into a spirit world where they can guide the dreams of the person who needs treatment. They show them things about themselves, and the plant spirits and animal totems help to repair the damage to the person's spirit body.

They have a remarkable success rate in treating a myriad of problems in this manner. One has to wonder when they share a hallucination of another world with someone else and can relate shared experiences, if this other world is a hallucination or if it is actually another realm of reality altogether. This other world is very real to both the shaman and the person who ingests the spirit of these plants.

Chakras

You can find this world with meditation also. The creator took small pieces of its divine energy, and gave them to every living creature. They are a part of every one of us, and they are known as chakras.

There are either seven or nine of them depending on the school of thought. I work with seven as I am a simple creature, and in the beginning it is hard enough to hold your focus long enough to even visualize all seven of them. I figure if there are an eighth and a ninth, I will find them eventually and they will make themselves known to me.

These chakras are located in your spine and head. I think of them like the colors of a rainbow. As you light them up, picture the light going through the ceiling and the trees and shining up into the atmosphere and thru the clouds, and down into the earth, connecting you to it.

The red is located at the base of your spine.

The Mantra is: Let my light go down into the earth, making the entire earth safe and solid and fortified by my light

Orange is located between your navel and groin.

The Mantra is: I will brighten the energy of everyone around me with the positive energy I send out to the world.

Yellow is located at the center of your mass, a few inches above your navel.

The Mantra is: My energy fills the world with strength, unity and security.

Green is your heart chakra, and is located behind your breast plate in the center of your chest.

The Mantra is: Peace love and joy radiate from me so that others feel their energy filled with it also when they are near me.

Blue is located in your throat.

The Mantra is: Let me be conscious of the words that I speak so that I may say the right thing at the right time.

Indigo or purple is located in your pineal gland, where your third eye is, in the middle of your forehead.

The Mantra is: Let me have the wisdom to see when I can best be of service to others.

White is the color of the crown chakra and is made up of all the colors of the rainbow, and connects you to your God source and higher self.

The Mantra is: I radiate peace and light up into the heavens and down into the earth with healing intent.

For now, just visualize these seven chakras. Don't worry about the mantras at first as they will come later as you get more familiar with the individual chakras. Your chakras all connect to different parts of the body. Bringing them all to a state of awareness will promote full body health. Each one activates a glandular system in the body that will help to invigorate you again.

I visualize my chakras as heavy stone balls, or faceted jewels, glowing with their irrespective colors. Some see cones that funnel the energy into your chakras. Some visualize the chakras opening like the petals of a lotus. Use whatever visualization you are most comfortable with.

As I concentrate on them I begin to get them spinning with my mind. They have weight and inertia to keep them spinning. As they spin they glow brighter and pulsate faster. I concentrate on each one for the space of three long, slow, full breaths, activating them and spinning them as I go.

Whole earth Healing

After I open all seven chakras I begin my healing meditation. I picture the river of love/light that flows through us and around us all. It is beautiful and golden and has the bright argent glare of molten steel ready to cast.

This river of light begins to rain down upon my head, and it has weight and mass. I can feel it beating upon my skull like a waterfall of pure love and light. It splashes off and falls all around me, covering my being in light. It is warm and comforting.

Suddenly this light comes through the top of my head, and floods into my being. I contain it inside me and let it quickly fill me up. My chakras are bathed in this pure love and light until I am full. I hold it in until I am ready to burst, and I let it out of me, to flood out in every direction, like a tidal wave of love and light going out in every direction from me like the shock wave of an instrument of destruction, but the exact opposite.

A wave of healing and love goes out over the world, sending love and healing in the places that need it the most. Places ravaged by war and nature alike. Places where there is pain, the love energy goes, and people come together in warm embraces. Dogs jump with glee as their masters come through the door.

Mother's faces light up as their child hands them a flower, and the child reflects this love back in delight at the mothers smile. Lovers look deep into one another's eyes and pull one another close.

The whales are leaping out of the sea, getting a small taste of our world much the same as we go into the water to get a taste of theirs. Barely able to pierce the veil, but taking great joy in it nonetheless.

I see my energy going out around the entire earth until it comes crashing together on the other side, and with love I hold the entire earth in my awareness. I put bandages of light on the places that hurt, covering places like Haiti, The Sudan, and the Middle East. I try to give every heart a little bit of that joy, and hold the Earth in my warm embrace for as long as I can.

As my focus tends to wander, I begin to pull that energy back into myself. I feel it coming back across the continents, across the oceans, the mountains, and the fields. I feel it coming back into myself, and I am rejuvenated with the power of that energy. I pull it into my Chi.

I see it light up from yellow to argent white, and I take that small ball of energy, and move it to parts of my body that need healing. It is spinning at a high rate, and pulsating so fast it is hardly noticeable. This ball of energy moves through my body, taking with it the pain and inflammation. It takes the bad cells that will cause cancer and disease, and it pulls them to it.

It comes out of my body and the spinning motion throws off this black energy and negativity, and it falls to the earth to be absorbed back into the All, where there is no such thing as bad energy, it is just energy.

I take this chi ball and go out searching along the energy pathways to my loved ones who need healing. I move it through their spirit bodies, and attempt to imprint that perfect ideal spirit body onto their imperfect physical package.

When I have exhausted myself, I pull this energy and awareness back into myself, and I consciously let the energy drain out of me, and I will each of my chakras to slow and close.

I usually sleep like a baby after spending a half hour or so doing my meditations. I liken it to lucid dreaming in many respects, but with much more control. Your mind can visualize anything, and with some meditation, your focusing skills will improve, and before you know it you will have dream-theater anytime you wish.

You may say you can't meditate, but if you just read that whole thing, you just went through your first guided meditation. The thing about meditation is that many people try to NOT think. This is simply impossible, and stilling your mind is something that comes with practice. You will notice I said stilling your mind, not quieting it. Holding your focus is the key.

Once you awaken to the simple connection you have to your chakras, your visualizations will change. Your connection to everything around you becomes much more profound, and you realize you are in no way separate from it all, but instead are one with everything. Everything comes from the mother, which is the living breathing and sentient planet that we are blessed to be experiencing this awareness on.

The mother comes from creator. All that we are and experience serves the creator. The consciousness learns and evolves as we react to the pain and the joy in our lives. All that is evil and vile is supposed to show us that we have a choice. We either embrace it or are repelled. We are very fortunate that most people are repelled.

The Chakras are small pieces of the divine consciousness, and as such, they are our direct connection to Creator. I have to add an addendum here, that finding your God source, though it may initially be a beautiful experience, does not come without some pain.

God does not show herself to you without first making you see and face your own self. This will come in some small glimmers of self realization at first. These hurt, but they are nothing compared to how it feels when you really have the proverbial scales removed from your eyes.

Before you actually get to your God source however, you have to face yourself. It hurts. Even if you consider yourself to be a good person, you may be shattered by the realizations of the impact you have on the world and those around you. You realize a transformation has begun, and you want to tell people.

Your experience is your own

You quickly realize that it is all your own, and that everyone around you has not suddenly gone through a change of spirit and embraced the thought of a higher power. Nobody shares your feelings, nor your excitement. Even people who love you will look at you as if you have silently slipped off the edge into the deep end. It is all your own.

So then you start to realize that words have an impact. Thoughts have an impact. Everything around us was born of thought, and it makes a difference. You are suddenly aware of how you walk on this earth, and who you hurt. Karma has meaning. Everything hurts as you go through that transformation, and you may cry and stomp your feet.

Some people cannot transform, and the experience slowly fades. If the experience is deep enough however, it starts the transformation process all on its own. A seed is planted and spirituality grows as a result. How much you change depends on your connection to your God source, whatever you call it. Like the bible says, the soil of some men's hearts is shallow and rocky, and nothing is going to bring them to spirit.

I once thought that was the soil of my own heart. Now that I have touched on my own God source, I am struggling with the transformation process. I feel like that old werewolf movie where he changes into this incredible creature, but it hurts during the transformation.

There is no growth without pain, and I will survive the pain of this change, and I will become who I really am. There is a point where a person is no longer studying to become a healer. You are transformed into one. It is a realization, and a threshold that you may cross without even knowing it. Suddenly you really are a healer in every sense of the word, and you have responsibility. The transformation is begun even before you realize it.

More meditation tips

I can't tell you enough that you need to meditate. Meditation hones your mind to hold an image and maintain focus. It vastly improves your visualization skills. If you have a hard time meditating I have a couple of simple things that may help.

As you meditate, put the soles of your feet together as well as the palms of your hands, as if you were going to say your nightly prayers. This aligns key energy points in your body and helps the flow of energy and helps you maintain good posture. Good posture is important for being able to maintain a meditative pose for any length of time.

If, like me, you have some extra weight, and you find yourself uncomfortable in this position, put a pillow under each knee to support the weight of your legs. This also raises your legs a bit and gives you a comfortable place to put your elbows as you maintain the prayer position. At first your side and support muscles will get tired quickly, so don't try to meditate too long. As you maintain your practice it will get longer and longer without your even willing it to do so.

You will come to look forward to the dream theater in your head at night. After a while you will not be able to go to sleep without satisfying your brains urge to play.

Start by getting into position, and relaxing. Breathe in to a 5 count and hold it for a five count and then breathe out to a five count. This simple repetition lulls your brain and helps quiet the babble in your head. It is also a simple mantra to use at first. I try to count just a little bit slower than my heart is beating, and my heartbeat quickly slows to the cadence of my mantra.

If this technique does not work for you, try visualizing the hands of a clock. Move the second hand around the clock at the proper intervals, counting slowly as you go. Your mind will automatically try to move all three hands of the clock at the same time. This is a lot for it to keep track of while it is counting, and forces the brain to multitask and distracts the babble in your head also.

I find I can reach a deep state fairly quickly using this technique. With practice your sessions will get longer, going from the 5-10 minutes that you will start out being able to hold focus, to some very relaxing 30-45 minute sessions where good visualization and concentration is employed throughout the meditation.

Many people may have a hard time maintaining focus for even the 5-10 minutes that are the base beginning of your meditation. Don't be discouraged and think it is impossible. The mind can be trained, even if it does resist at first. It will slowly come into line and your meditations will improve.

I find it very easy to meditate on the world I live in and my profound connection to it all. I always try to include some Whole Earth Energy Healing in my practice. Mother Earth needs this love and healing. She is sick and in pain, and she is bound to get worse before the human race as a whole wakes up.

I believe, as does my teacher, that getting others to join with us, that just possibly we can shift this paradigm from the ever perpetuating war machine we have going towards a more spiritual world where the rulers have no secrets and we have nothing to fight about because we all recognize one another's perfect right to live and exist as we see fit. I visualize a world where prisons are obsolete because everyone knows what it feels like to be both the aggressor and the victim.

I see a world where the word of God is revered and sacred, and used as neither a weapon nor an excuse to wage a holy war, nor draw lines in the sand. I see a world where animals don't have to suffer terrible existences to satisfy our urge for fast food.

I see a world where people truly love and appreciate one another for the individuals they are and not hurt one another for their differences. I can see this. When I do my energy healing this is what I visualize for the entire world.

The old Native American elders used to sit and visualize the beautiful world they wanted for their grandchildren. It has been proven that a handful of monks can lower crime rates in high crime neighborhoods simply by meditating on peace for that area. These men are enlightened souls, who have spent their entire lives searching for spirit and enlightenment.

The thing is, you don't have to be a Zen master to do this meditation. All you have to do is practice and focus your awareness, and you become almost as effective as a Zen master, and you really can work with the force. Things you would think miraculous become possible.

Chi or "The Force"

The force, as portrayed in the classic Star Wars series, is actually real. Human beings can manipulate reality and bend it to suit our needs. There are police forces in China that carry no weapon but a bottle of water charged with their own Chi. If someone acts up, they simply remove the cap and dash water on the person, who is often knocked unconscious to the ground.

Martial arts experts are not using the delicate bones of their hands to break huge chunks of ice or concrete with explosive force that would be hard for a strong man with a sledgehammer to duplicate. The bones of the hands alone are just not capable of sustaining that much force. It is the mastery of Chi or vital energy that helps that hand do the explosive work for him.

This same explosive energy can be used to heal, or to ease aches and inflammation. It can knit broken bones together, and shrink tumors. You can use it on yourself or others equally well. It is as malleable as your thoughts and as big as you believe it to be.

It is the river of love light that flows through all things. It connects us and transmits thoughts and images for us. It is what makes you slam on your brakes right before you would have gotten T-boned at the intersection. It is the connection that enables mother's intuition and ESP. One day with science and mathematics, they will suddenly find the equation, and the supernatural will become the commonplace. Maybe they already have and we just don't know it yet.

What we do know is that we all need for something to change. I can feel a quickening as I have heard it described. The beat is picking up, and things are happening in the world which will alter the course of our destiny for the better or worse.

All of us working together can effect change. We need a gradual shift of the paradigm, not a revolution, and the way I see it this country is heading for one if we don't somehow alter the path. I believe creator uses the collective energy we are putting off to build our current reality for us, second by second, and that the collective energy in the world must be getting very negative for all these things to be happening at once.

We all need for this to change, for down that path lies doom in all the classic sense of the words. This world has gotten out of control. We have become instead of the beacon of freedom and opportunity, the country that tortures and thumbs our nose at international law.

Despite the improvements touted in the media, this country is in a downward spiral. Our own Federal Reserve has printed money out of thin air and bought up 90% of the US debt. This is not good, people. We are caught up in a perpetual war we cannot win, and have troops spread out all over the world forcing our way of life on people at gunpoint in the name of "freedom" while we are the country who has the most of its own people locked in prisons.

Our current energy output is responsible for the current state of our reality. Every thought you think and every word you speak goes out on the grid, and it is either harmonic or discordant depending on the intent.

You can take yourself anywhere with these meditations. Modify them and grow them to suit your needs. Heal the woes in our own country as well as those in the rest of the world. Use them to help you get away from the frustration and aggression we all encounter in our daily lives. Working together we can change this paradigm using our focused energy to heal the world, and ourselves by extension.

As you meditate, you may find yourself drawn into the negative aspects of your life and experiences. Your mind will dredge up these things and show them to you in living color. These things have to be dealt with before you can find inner peace in your meditations. These things draw off your vital energy like an arterial bleed.

You have to heal yourself as well as others. Forgiving is a big part of that.

Forgiving

Forgiveness comes very hard in some cases. It is very hard to really forgive yourself. It is very hard to forgive someone who really wronged you. Someone may have seriously injured you physically or spiritually, or possibly someone you love. There are victims out there that may never find it in themselves to really forgive the sin done to them.

You have to somehow find it in yourself to heal that wound nonetheless. Time and love will cover it in a protective bandage after you take it out and examine it in detail. Your meditations will inevitably take you there sooner or later, so I feel it is best to get your self-healing done first. I am still working on that one myself. It's a tough one for sure.

You may be a soldier who has been asked to do terrible things for the greater good of all and be dealing with the PTSD that naturally comes from having a heart and being involved in war. Some soldiers go through this trauma and come out with no guilt whatsoever and some suffer from it the rest of their lives.

You can heal these wounds by forgiving yourself and knowing that you can do some positive things for the world regardless of your past. Forgiving yourself is a gradual thing, not something that happens overnight. Even if you consider yourself unscathed, you suffered every time you hurt someone else whether you acknowledge that in your waking life or not.

You can repay your own conscience every time you make a positive thing happen in the world. Everything you do and think balances those scales of karma back towards finding the inner peace we all deserve. Time heals all these wounds, but you have to heal your soul with positive actions. Every single one reinforces the fact that you have value and are still a positive force in the world.

It can be very hard to look at old wounds, and as we look at Huna Shamans, you will learn about the energy strings that attach all of us to one another.

You can break those attachments with visualization, and close that hole in your energy field, even if it is a temporary fix at first, it gets habitual, and with practice those wounds get harder and harder to find the pain in. That energy is once again your own to use for yourself. The healing will have begun for real.

That is the beauty of meditation. Your mind has the ability to heal yourself. I went for years without more than a two day case of the sniffles because every time I felt a cold coming on I visualized my body fighting it and just killing it off with white light blood cells, like the white knight heroes of old, galloping through my blood veins killing off that dis-ease.

That is what disease is in the body, it is dis-ease. Many problems can be eased simply by forgiving yourself and letting go of the guilt that is making us soul sick. Much depression and anxiety can be helped with self forgiveness. None of us have been perfect in this earthly package.

We were not supposed to be. We and the creator learn from our mistakes. We also grow and evolve from every single one. Some of us are knuckleheads, and have to be hit on the head over and over again before the message sinks in. Some of us never do get it and go through our lives damaging people everywhere we go with complete impunity.

We are all supposed to learn from them too. The creator is behind every pair of eyes you look into. Creator is in every face. Every breath and word and thought creates a vibratory resonance that goes out on the great grid of energy that connects us all.

Anger, depression, sadness, pain, loneliness, these things go out on the grid as a static and disruptive noise, that puts stress and negativity into the creative energy. Your thoughts go out from you like a ripple in still water. (Thank you Jerry)

Love, smiles, kind words and gentle thoughts go out on this grid like a beautiful chord being strummed on the world's biggest harp. These vibrations go much farther and have much more resonance than the static of negativity. One drop of love dispels an ocean of negativity.

It just doesn't take much to effect a change for the positive. All you have to do is start the thought process that you want to do it, and remember that it is your thoughts as well as your actions and words that make a difference.

If you can't change your thought process then it is all for naught. Your unconscious is like an unruly child. Gentle guidance away from negative thoughts and guilt is the way. When you have changed your thought process and begun to train your mind away from negativity, you will have begun to transform into the spiritual creature we are all destined to become.

This can be a hard process. With practice it will work for all of us though, and our minds can be gently persuaded to focus on the beauty in this world. It is all around us. You will find you appreciate the little things so much more when you start to connect with the natural world around you. This world is full of beauty and love, all you have to do is look around and open your heart to it.

Guilt is the most worthless and yet the most persistent of human emotions. Guilt rides you like a parasite, and accomplishes absolutely nothing. The past is the past, and it is OK to feel regret. You need to learn to leave it at that and stop beating yourself over the head with past inadequacies and actions.

Yesterday is not tomorrow, and there is no reason in the world that tomorrow cannot be a better day regardless of your situation as you see it right now. If you are still alive to think about change, there is still time to affect it. Guilt is the great enemy when developing your spirit and energy.

Like everything in our reality, change begins with a thought. The habit of meditating for change in the world is an easy one to get into. I do it like my evening prayers. You have to try not to focus on images of the pain and bad things in the world, but instead to concentrate on the beautiful world you envision that you would be proud to pass off to your children.

If I find myself getting stuck in negativity and the pain around me in the world, I tend to just stop meditating for that night. I don't really care to transmit that out into the grid, but then other times it can connect me and make me feel that all is right with the world. Use your own judgment if you are just putting out depression and anger, or if you can pull it together with thoughts of love and peace and healing.

I often find that performing the visualizations of my healing can pull me outside myself and bring me peace if I find myself in troubled waters. I have found it a great tool for my occasional depression that comes from the harsh ways of the world around me and feeling inadequate to the tasks that I need to do just to take care of my daily life.

Meditation can pull me back on the track, and if I do it early in the day, it can change the course of what would have been a bad day from my own individual concerns and troubles. It soothes my mind no matter what my mental state.

When I meditate I visualize a flow of energy circulating around my torso from my base chakra up my spine and down the front of my body and back up my spine again in a continuous flow. Gathering energy can help you to increase your personal energy level and feel this flow to a greater extent.

How to Gather Earth Energy

This works best outside, but I often to it indoors with my feet on the floor and just visualize my energy connecting to the earth through the bottoms of my feet. If you do it outdoors, it is best performed with the soles of your feet on the Earth.

Stand with your feet at shoulder width. Put your hands together in the prayer position, palms together. Visualize the Earth Energy running through the bottom of your feet and up the back of your legs.

It meets at your base chakra, and begins to either go up the front of you and down the back (usually for a female) or up the back of your spine along your chakras, and then back down the front of you. (For a male)

I visualize this energy coming up my legs meeting at my base chakra and charging up my chakras as it travels up my spine, over the top of my head where I breathe it in and send it back down the front of my chakras, energizing them all.

Then it once again goes down my legs and back into the earth. The point is to feel the circulation of this energy along the chakras, and visualize it energizing them and you.

You can channel this energy so it flows thru all the chakras or just circulate it in the lower three chakras to create a different sort of energy that can be channeled into more dynamic actions, such as the more explosive movements of martial arts.

Focus on the life giving energy taken in with each breath and then visualize it moving where you want it to go. As you breathe out, focus on positively charging your own aura or energy body with this life energy.

Visualize it building in your base chakra then see it energizing all the chakras slowly going from bottom to top. The energy is lighting them up bright and strong. This energy needs applied somewhere and you can do many things with it.

You should spend some time channeling this vital energy into building up your light body or actual spirit. I visualize my light body as a huge version of the perfect me that towers over me and shines with an inner luminosity so bright it can burn the negative energy away from me. He is a warrior of light that can overcome any dark energy out there.

Having a strong light body has a direct effect on the physical body also as this is your own spirit. You can build and strengthen it so that when your time comes, you will be better able to pass over and retain who you were through the process of leaving this world.

When I do a cleansing, I visualize this light warrior burning the negativity out of every corner of the house I am cleansing with the searing white light of love and peace and joy, and print that love/peace/joy into every corner of the house in place of that negativity. Any bad energy is vaporized and falls back to the earth in its elemental form to be absorbed and made anew.

Not all spirits can be gotten rid of that easy, but most of them won't stay when confronted with that light and love. The negative ones need fear and anger to feed on. Once you improve your mental state, they will lose interest and go elsewhere, and you may find yourself attracting positive energy instead. Having spiritual love and light around is never a bad thing.

I believe as you increase your light output that suddenly you show up on the spiritual radar, and as you build a practice your vibration goes up and maybe you are more able to tune in to them also.

I don't know if it holds true as a rule or not but I think that spiritual activity increases as you become more perceptive and you had better find a way to incorporate that into your belief system and be prepared to deal with it. Fortune favors the prepared mind in more ways than one.

Spend some time creating a space in your head to go to when you meditate. Decorate your mental place as you would like it to be the most peaceful and Zen place you can imagine. I go to a place decorated in rich reds, burgundies, and gold. It is a comfortable place where I can lay back and find myself dreaming within the dream.

You can go to a beach, or fly to the top of the highest mountain. You can fly your perception amongst the tops of the firs and pines and swoop down low into the Grand Canyon gazing down on the Colorado River.

You can put yourself into the body of a hawk and look out through its eyes and feel the wind in the feathers of its face. Taste its breath. Run through the jungle looking out through the eyes of a jaguar. Take yourself home and walk the streets of your youth, or go hang gliding or jump from place to place like Spring Heel Jack, all in your mind without going anywhere.

You can do anything once you learn to focus your perception. It quickly becomes something you look forward to every night.

Breathing and how to do it effectively

A few words about breathing in general are called for here I think. To take a full breath, first you breathe in until your lungs are full. Now straighten up and pull your shoulders back and breathe in some more, filling your lungs all the way to the top and bottom. Hold that breath for a few seconds, then breathe out.

When you think your lungs are empty, use your diaphragm to push all the rest of the air out of your lungs so they are really empty. From there you can refresh all the air in your lungs with good fresh air and chi, and when you do a few breaths like this in the morning it will really rejuvenate and invigorate you to start your day, or help get oxygen to your brain for good meditation also.

In a very short time you will feel the difference in your physical energy level as the air you breathe in oxygenates the entire body and allows all the cells throughout to have the energy they need to perform their biological functions more efficiently.

As you begin to breathe more deeply on a regular basis it really helps if you try to maintain proper posture and stand straight up shoulders back and with your head directly above your shoulders. Most people begin to slouch as they get older, and the head gradually moves forward on the more relaxed neck, which causes inflammation and pain in the neck and shoulders that so many people suffer from.

Simply retraining your muscles to support proper posture will help you to feel much better as you age, and this is not meant to tell anyone to try to do something they may not be able to do if they are physically unable.

This is more for people that are getting to that age where everything starts to hurt. If you can learn these simple habits you will feel better and be more mobile as you get older.

The thing about these visualizations is that you do what works best for you. If the energy feels better going the opposite way from what I say, by all means do what your mind can wrap around the easiest. That is why I will cover several ways to do it, so you can take what works for you and put together your own visualization system.

You can hang on to this energy if you want to simply by picturing it charging up your chakras. I tend to sort of clench my posterior like I am trying not to let anything bad escape, but instead I picture holding this energy inside me and charging my own energy field with it. This seems particularly effective when you are tired if done along with the proper deep breathing technique. The full yogic breath oxygenates and rejuvenates you even if you are exhausted.

When you hang on to this energy it can be applied in healing techniques through visualization or the actual laying on of hands. You can use it to form chi balls, and empower your prayers, as the hunas believe. Empowered prayer is a powerful tool once you start to use it.

Here is a simple test to do to prove your energy radiance. Find a partner, and the both of you rub your palms together briskly and feel the heat produced by the friction. This is energy you are producing with this simple motion.

Now hold your hands a few inches apart, and feel that energy between your palms. Visualize it, you can almost see it. Feed it with your mind, and make it grow.

Move your hands a few more inches apart, and feel the heat energy expand, and warm your palms again. Use your mind and your energy field to feed this chi energy, and keep growing it bigger, until your hands are about two feet apart. Now put your hands out towards your partner, who should be about 4 feet away from you, palms out towards one another.

Feel the heat of one another's energy fields warming your palms still. Now both of you take a step back, feeding and growing the energy between you and feel the energy still warming your palms the same as when your hands were four inches apart and still hot from the friction.

You can step apart until you are filling the room with your energy fields. Remember you are as big as you think you are. Your palms will still be feeling that spirit heat that you generated. That is a simple demonstration just to show you your energy is there. You can learn to do anything from warm your hands to ease your loved ones pains, to actual healing, to learning to read a book with your energy field.

Muscle Testing

Some time should be spent on how to check if the energy you are circulating is affecting you in a positive or a negative manner. This can be done with muscle testing. First a baseline is needed.

To do this by yourself make a circle with your first finger and thumb, and try to pull it open with the other hand. Remember the force it takes to pull your finger and thumb apart.

If you have a partner, stand with your arm extended out parallel to the floor, and have your partner push down gently at the wrist with two fingers as you resist.

After doing energy circulation work try this muscle test again, and see if the energy had a strengthening or a weakening effect. If the energy had a weakening effect, try circulating the energy in the opposite direction.

These muscle tests are important, as improperly working with your chi energy has been known to cause psychosis in some individuals. This is not a game, and the chi energy and Kundalini energy are real phenomenon, and not just something you may have read about.

As you build on this energy and learn to manipulate it, your mind will become more focused and you will change for the better. You will "tune in" to a much greater extent than you ever thought possible.

Gathering Sky energy

To pull energy down from the sky, I stand first with my hands together in the prayer form, and I visualize the argent white light of creation raining down on my head with weight and mass. I can feel it falling on me like a warm waterfall. I breathe in this chi energy through my nose. I direct this energy up along the top of my skull, and then down the front of my chakras to my base, and around and back up the back of my chakras and over the top of my head, and take it back into my nose, circulating it along this path faster and faster, and holding this energy inside me.

Once I am charged with this energy, I can direct it for healing, either interpersonal or long distance. I extend my arms and reach out as far around me as I can and scoop this energy directly into my third chakra, or sometimes each chakra gets some time spent charging it separately.

My own chi is then added to by the chi that is all around us. I can send this chi energy anywhere by the simple fact of my awareness. Science has proven that awareness changes reality. I can affect anything I can think of. You are truly as big as you believe yourself to be.

When you send healing and love out into the world, you are affecting change. Your very intent is heard by the creative energy, and you are for that short time adding that drop of love that is dispelling the black negativity and hatred in the world.

Your awareness is felt and the change is a real one. If a handful of monks can lower crime rates in a violent inner city, imagine what would happen if we had a global move towards healing.

Now you know how to gather energy from the earth and sky. This is a first step in using the chi energy, and building it up within yourself so you can use it to help heal others. As you meditate and gather this energy, intent is very important. I start every meditation with intent, whether it is to still my mind for sleep or to gather energy for healing.

Performing either of these exercises during times of energetic weather, such as when a thunderstorm is blowing up, or when the wind is really whipping or at sunrise or sunset can have some very impressive results that are quite palpable with very little practice.

As you get more focused on the breathing, the chi energy will improve. The key to life and chi is the breath, and focusing awareness on taking in positive energy with each breath and dispelling your own negative energy with each exhale is what chi is all about.

As you grow, your own negativity will not be as apparent, and you will not have to dispel it all the time. In these times you are breathing out positive energy into your environment as you exhale.

Changes

First it will positively charge your own energy field. You will notice positive changes throughout your life. People will respond differently to you, and you may find yourself in a different position than you had at first thought.

Eventually if you continue in a positive shift, your whole environment will become more positively charged. You will be on the path to becoming a more spiritual and connected person. This chi energy plants the seeds of this change, and if you keep working with it you will see it manifest throughout your life.

Eventually people will start to seek you out as they come to expect this positive reinforcement. It is such a rare thing in the world we live in right now that it takes people by surprise when you are being a positive force instead of a negative one.

Huna

Some words on Polynesian Huna. Some folks of the Christian faith may have a problem with Huna. This is because Huna utilizes working with spirit. However the spirit that the Huna works with is his own lower and higher spirits.

The Huna believe that you are made up of three spirits. The Uhane, which is the lower self and responsible for your base instincts and animal urges. It is the source of addictions and impulse decisions. The Uhane is like a child that only wants what it wants, but it can be guided, and is in contact with the higher self. The Uhane is also the source of the energy strings that connect us all through our awareness.

The Amaqua is higher self and the source of your connection to God, and is the seat of your wisdom and power. The Amaqua can help you in controlling that little voice in your head that says all those negative things. Ask for help from your Higher self, and see if it doesn't help to quiet that negative voice in your head.

The Unahipilli is the self in the present, and is guided by the lower and higher selves. Often if the person is prone to addictions or alcoholism, the lower self is controlling this person, and he is living in his base urges for immediate gratification. The Higher self can help with that too.

Connection to the lower and higher selves can be established with a pendulum. Almost anything will work, a set of keys on a string, a favored crystal or pendant, simply suspended between the first and middle finger and the thumb, suspended long enough that it can swing freely.

You start by asking your pendulum to show you a yes answer and then a no answer. When you have established which is which you will have a mode of communication between you and your higher and lower selves.

For me a front to back motion is yes, a side to side motion is no if I am addressing my lower self, and diagonally one way or the other is the same from my higher self. Round in circles means I don't know.

Next you ask the pendulum out loud if you are communicating with your own lower self, the one and only lower self born to me in this world, and no other. If you get a yes answer, ask if there are any other entities or energies attached to you besides the lower self.

If you find that there are entities attached, say out loud, "I hereby revoke any permissions or access granted by me or my higher or lower selves for you to be here, and I ask you to leave my energy field."

Ask again, if this is your own lower self, and if there are entities attached still. You should get a no answer, but there may be persistent energies attached to you through the loss of a loved one or trauma you may have been through that may require some help in removing. You can ask through the pendulum for help from your higher self or your god source for help in removing these entities. Communication with the higher self can be established through the pendulum in the same manner.

When a dialogue has been established with the higher and lower selves, questions about all facets of your life can be asked and answered. Guidance can be there for the asking. I was a tad skeptical of the pendulum practice until I practiced it a few times. Now I have the odd sensation that something is tweaking the string of my pendulum in the middle and forcing it into motion in answer to my words.

When I first contacted my higher self I received a rush of satisfaction that came from an unknown source. It was as if I was relieved to be in contact with myself finally. It is an interesting process, and worth the investment of time and energy to practice with until you get more comfortable with the process.

I speak aloud to my higher self for help when I do long distance healing. The Huna believed we are all attached by energy strings that emanate from the lower belly to everyone we are aware of or have interacted with.

They believe you can follow these energy strings to the people you want to heal (or harm) and work with their own vital energies long distance.

The Huna had a death prayer that was much feared. If the Huna wished you harm, he simply prayed for your death, and within days you would start to die.

Max Freedom Long wrote a book called The Secret Science behind the Miracles, in which he talked about scoffing at a Huna, and in a very short time becoming so sick with some unknown malady, he begged for the prayer to be recalled, which it was, and he got better. He also talks about a huna who was able to regrow a missing limb for a man.

The huna work with your spirit body, which contains a perfect representation of what you are supposed to be, and they imprint this perfect spirit body on the sick physical body, and heal it in this manner. You have to wonder why the only office of the Catholic inquisition still open today is in the Polynesian islands, and directly opposed to these Hunas.

Empowered Prayer

The Empowered prayer is another facet of Huna which I adhere to. To do an empowered prayer, you simply form a chi ball between your hands, circulating energy into it. You will feel your hands warm like they are in the noonday sun when you get adept at it. As you form this chi ball, you simply visualize and feel and believe what it is that you want to happen, like it already had.

Feel it, believe it. Know it to be real and be grateful for whatever change you have manifested, and then send that ball of energy out into the ether with that prayer (belief) and feel it to be already true. That core belief is the essence of empowered prayer and manifestation.

Once again, intent is very important, and keeping focus on your prayer subject is also important. Meditating regularly can help you to keep the focus you need to become proficient with this method. Focusing your mind to your intent is a powerful thing, and can help you in many facets of your life.

Some words on Healing Native style. This is as close to the way we did this as I can remember, and if I got anything wrong or omitted anything, I apologize. This was included because it was where spirit came to me and I have been on the path ever since. I am very grateful for the lessons and the struggles.

A Beautiful Healing Experience

Before I start on this information I wish to say that I included this information to be approached with the utmost respect to sacred traditions and that the ritual described here is as close as I can relate it from the experiences I had personally and are not intended to reflect any form of disrespect to anybody or any sacred beliefs. I do not pretend to be initiated by any of them, and I came by my knowledge through many sources through the years.

Please forgive me in advance if I say anything that does not match the ceremony you perform as we all approach the creator in our own way and I mean no disrespect.

The Native American Shamans pray to many spirits. They include Wakan Tanka or Creator, or the animal totems, the spirits of the four directions, and Mother Earth and Grandmother Moon, tree spirits, stone spirits, and spirits in almost everything. Healing is done with the assistance of these spirits, and the persons own spirit.

The practice of Inipi, or Sweat Lodge is also very important to most of the native people. This is a cleansing and healing process in which you enter into a small lodge, usually made of bent branches tied together into a dome, and covered with hides, or in modern times a dark opaque canvas that totally blocks the light. It could be a hollow made in the earth. Any structure to keep out all light and keep in the heat from the heated stones will do.

The ceremony is simple and similar in most tribes. First you prepare the lodge, which is a days work in itself, as there is an altar, and a fire pit and a walking path to the lodge which must be made clean in a ceremonial manner.

First a large pile of stones is gathered. Enough for four rounds are gathered. Care is used to make sure they have no cracks or fissures as these may explode when heated in the fire and send shrapnel flying that can injure a fire keeper.

Usually one person is picked to be a fire keeper, and he is responsible for the stacking and ceremonial heating of the stones and wood. He also stays outside the lodge and prays and watches over the people inside until they call for more stones at which time he gets up and removes the antlers from some medicine water and gets rocks from the fire that have been superheated in the fire for hours.

The wood and stones are stacked together so that when it burns down the stones will be in a huge pile of coals to achieve maximum heating. Different tribes do it slightly different but usually a ceremonial "gate or door" is created at the four directions, and the fire is started by four "gate keepers" on all four sides simultaneously as prayers are said.

Everyone who is to sweat participates in some manner. Someone splits the wood, and prayer ties are made by all in different colored pieces of cloth with a small tobacco offering. All tools to be used like the maul to split the wood with and the scissors to cut the prayer tie cloths must be smudged over a bed of sage or cedar to purify them before use.

Fellowship and snacks and lots of fluids are taken in before the sweat, as you lose a lot of water in the lodge. As the ceremony begins, each person circles the fire pit, and says prayers as they go, for what they wish to accomplish in the lodge.

Precious or sacred objects like medicine bags are not worn in the lodge as heat can damage stones in the bag, so the sacred objects are placed on the altar with more prayers.

The person proceeds up the prayer path and at the door of the lodge, they pray aloud to the spirits of the four directions, turning to face each one. Then you go backwards into the lodge.

Some tribes of course don't worry which direction they go in, but where I have sweated, you go in and go to the left, and go around as far as you can, and sit down. Sometimes there are a lot of people crammed into a small space, and sometimes there are two lines or more of people around the inside of the lodge. The ones closest to the fire can have a hot night.

As the wood burns down, the stones are taken from the fire on deer antlers that are soaked in water so they don't burn. They are brought individually into the lodge by the fire keeper, and each one is welcomed by all the people. The stone is set in a shallow depression in the center of the lodge.

The Shaman or person conducting the sweat has a bucket of prepared water with many medicines soaking in it, like lavender, cedar, pinion pine, sage, tobacco, and others depending on where you are at. He dashes the water on the hot stones with a cedar bough, saying prayers to the stone people and the spirits of the four directions as the stones are brought in.

Ancestors and helper and healing animal spirits are invited in, and all dark spirits are requested to leave. Songs are sung as the stones are brought in, drums and tambourines and rattles are played. Native songs passed down through the generations are shared, along with more contemporary music that everyone plays along and sings along with. It is a joyous time, and I have had tears stream down my face from the power of the spirit in the lodge.

When all the stones are in, and the heat is almost unbearable, the door is closed, and complete and utter blackness envelops you. The only light is the red hot stones glowing dimly in the center, and they quickly cool enough to lose their meager light. More medicines and water is dashed on the stones, making the steam thick so that if you blow gently on yourself it burns like fire.

One would think that you would quickly grow weary of it like you do in a sauna, but it is different somehow. The sweat and toxins run out of you in rivers, and you would think that everyone would come out stinking like a wet horse, but you come out clean and refreshed.

When the steam is thick as it can get, a talking stick is passed around, and the only person who may talk is the person holding the stick. Each person passes the stick around and talks about issues in their life that they need to fix, or things that no longer serve them, or any issue that is bothering you in your life, depending on what round it is.

Four rounds of the talking stick are observed, with a different purpose for each round. Depending on how many and how long winded they are, you can be in the inipi for up to three hours or more. A break is taken between each round, and people go out into the cold night air in their shorts and towel, or buck naked in some lodges. Drinks are had between each round to keep hydration levels up. Each person prays again before they re-enter the lodge for the next round.

It gets very hot, and you are in the lodge for an extended period of time sometimes, so it is nothing to be ashamed of to "go to earth" or lay down where the air is slightly cooler.

Often a good meal and more fellowship follow a good sweat. It is refreshing and rejuvenating and good for the soul in general. Often in the lodge spirit lights and shades can be seen. My wife has seen full blown apparitions of an old man sitting in front of the man who runs the Inipi I sweated in, on more than one occasion in the lodge there were spirit orbs.

My first spiritual awakening happened in a Sweat Lodge, and it is a powerful healing tool. This is where the scales were removed from my own eyes and is why this was included in the book.

You don't have to be Native American to sweat. A lodge can be built anywhere and out of anything. I have a friend with a Cadillac sweat lodge with nice padded benches and all.

More of a fancy steam room with a fire pit outside, but it works the same way. Total light deprivation is important in my opinion, in order for your mind to be on full alert and allow you to take in the wonders of the Inipi. I find the experience to be as beneficial for the mind as it is for the body. Almost like an enforced meditation.

Vision Quest

A quest for vision is undergone for many reasons. Sometimes it is done to find ones animal totems. Sometimes it is for guidance in a personal issue. Sometimes just to see what there is to see. There are a few different varieties of vision quest.

Some do it through deprivation and fasting, some through the use of plant medicines. Here I will cover the deprivation and fasting, and leave the plant medicines for later, as that deserves a book all of its own.

A vision quest is approached in a humble and ceremonial manner. A place must be prepared where the vision quester will not be bothered so they can pursue their visions.

A place is prepared with a small shelter, and many prayer ties are made in the days prior as the preparations are done. The prayer ties are arranged on and around the shelter, and a small altar is assembled for more prayer during the vision quest.

The quester goes out to sit. He sits there for up to four days, with no food and only a small bottle of water if that. He is exposed to the elements as all he has is an elemental shelter. Sunburn may ensue if care is not chosen for a location. The first day your stomach churns and gurgles as it processes the last of the food, and some hunger pangs begin.

The second day you are in misery, tired of sitting there, your stomach is thinking you abandoned it, and your guts are cramping trying to squeeze the last of the food through. Your mouth is parched and your lips are dry, and your tongue sticks to the roof of your mouth.

The third day your body is more at rest. You have found a stone to suck on to generate some spit to swallow. You wait and watch for a vision, saying prayers throughout for the vision you seek. You may have some serious hunger pangs indeed now.

The 4th day, you find an odd sort of lucidity as your body starts to dissolve itself. Your hunger pangs have passed. You feel like you could go days with no food. You may or may not be more inclined to have a vision in this state. Sometimes you have to look back at your time out on the hill and examine it closely to find the true meaning.

Sometimes you may be left wondering what it was all about, but if you keep seeking you will find eventually.

Prayer

Prayer is a very powerful thing in any form. It is the very embodiment of the creative human mind focusing with intent and will. Christians pray to God to create their intent. They assume a position similar to a meditative pose with their hands together, putting their hands together and knowingly or not connecting the chakras of their hands and connecting energy meridians in their bodies.

Catholics pray to saints and the Mother Mary to fulfill their creative needs in much the same way, with ceremony and ritual lighting of candles, and taking in of the blood and flesh of Christ.

Voodoo practitioners and Santa Ria priests also perform rituals and let blood in order to further their prayer creations, praying to a higher power, in the guise of familiar spirits and papa Legba, known by many names as the opposite of the light.

The Native Americans pray to the higher spirits of earth and sky and creator, as well as animal spirits to fulfill their needs. Everyone looks to someone, or at least most of us do. The similarity here is the focused intent of the human mind to change our reality through what some would think of as miraculous means.

The fact is that we DO create our own reality. Prayer is simply the focused intent of the human brain attempting to change reality. Prayer is thought, and everything on this earth that didn't grow here spontaneously is born of thought. We are part of the creator on this world, and we are powerful creators in our own right. Look around you at what we have created with the power of our thought.

Everything you see around you was born of human thought and manifested into reality by the energy we all put out to make it what it is. The combined will and focus of the human brain is without limits. The beautiful thing about our intelligence is its need and ability to overcome any and all obstacles.

The modern educational system

Our educational system now is set up in a way that trains the uniqueness out of us. From the time you set foot in a public school now you are told to conform to an image.

Instead of being taught to seek a passion, students are taught that to achieve you must pass the tests. To make your goal you must pass the tests, the same tests everybody else has to pass, or you are considered a failure, and sent to remedial school where you can learn to pass that test. The inspiration and passion is bred out of a student in this system.

This system does not embrace the wide spectrum of specialties to be found in the incredible human animal. Instead it makes us all aspire to be the same, to pass those same tests and get that same knowledge with no leeway given for creative specialty or genius that is outside the given parameters.

Anyone who sees things in a different way is scoffed at and ridiculed by the group at large. This system sets certain students up to fail. Students that may very well have their own passions and skills in a slightly different set of parameters, but in the status quo system we have now, they fall to the wayside as being unable to "pass the test".

In school my daughter was falling behind and was considered lazy because she wanted to draw pictures all day. We saw this and simply kept the kid in art supplies. Now she is a successful graphic artist who gets paid for her work. Better than flipping hamburgers somewhere as most young kids end up doing.

Imagination and fantasy are suppressed. Kids are taught that there is no real magic in the world and that Harry Potter is as close as they are going to get to real magic.

The real magic is inside of every one of us. We can heal both ourselves and others. We can manifest our own reality and create things from our thoughts into our reality. We are all magicians and creators in our own right. We were given this ability early on, and the modern paradigm has beaten it out of us.

It is our destiny to find this again, and I believe that as more people awaken to the creative powers within us, this paradigm will change and ever so slowly, the balance will shift back towards the center, towards Love and Spirit.

The paradigm now is to make money and pay money. It is becoming more and more obvious that this paradigm cannot sustain itself. It will fail.

When it does, this world will be in a state of flux as a new paradigm begins. These could be very tumultuous times as the old rulers try to keep their positions and the new paradigm becomes more obvious.

During these times, the focus of the people towards spirit will shift the balance either more towards the center or away from it depending on how many people can open themselves to the reality of their abilities and make some positive change in their lives.

It is like the old Lakota story that there are two dogs in every man's heart, a black dog and a white dog, and they are always fighting one another. The one that wins is the one that you feed the most.

Our Motivations are important. Think about it. What motivates you to do the things you do? What makes any of us do the things we do, from expressing love to hate, drive or lethargy, Imagination or realism. When I think about what motivates me, I come down to the experience. The experience of every single moment, realized.

Some people have incredible drive and are able to move mountains in their lifetimes. The trick is to find a direction that gives you passion. Then you can pour your whole life and essence into it and move that mountain.

Some people collect more money than they will ever be able to spend in a lifetime, and still they have a drive to have more, to acquire more. It will never be enough.

Still they have a need inside of them that is not satisfied and will not be satisfied. It is insatiable, because nothing in this material world can fill it. It is not something you can put in your pocket.

What are your motivations in reading this book? What drives you to spend precious parts of your life looking at words on pages? The drive for knowledge and fulfillment is insatiable and primordial. Its roots lie deep in our energy consciousness because we are here to experience the material world in all its glory and ugliness, and we have the primordial genetic disposition to seek and experience both sides of the yin and the yang.

In the modern world we live in there is not much chance for spirituality. The religious path is becoming less and less a mainstream way of life in this sex and drugs society. Catholicism has had its image cast in a questionable light. Christianity is not as strictly adhered to as it once was and is being reflected badly in modern media. The media are portraying people who have faith in their God as fringe groups clinging to their guns and bibles in this more possession oriented society.

This country is becoming a non spiritual nation based in the acquisition of material possessions that do nothing to enhance the spirituality of the owner. Our entertainment is made up of mindless drivel. There is nothing that challenges the mind to consider the implications of right and wrong. There is no rite of passage to assure one's honor.

So my motivation is to experience. All of it, pain, love, life, death, rain, and sunshine, all are part of the wheel, and part of the experience we signed on to go through for the growth of the consciousness. Every scar you have is testament to that experience.

Every breath you breathe is filled with the life essence that enables you to have that experience. Every kiss, every touch, every blow you strike, it is all part of the life experience that helps the consciousness to grow. What do you strive for? What will you fight for?

The two paradigms

At the moment there are two main paradigms in play here. On the one hand there are the money people, the mega corporations that are quietly ruling the chaos that is the world through the enslavement of the people through a monetary system that does not compensate the people at its base with a living wage, forcing them to work their lives away just to have a place to live. This is the never ending war machine that has to be fed with the blood and sweat of the people.

On the other hand are people trying to live more in harmony with Mother Earth. There are people that are not behind the war machine and want to find a way for all of us to live together and help one another through love and understanding to make this world a better more peaceful place. These two paradigms are like that black and white dog in every man's heart.

Somehow we have to feed that white dog, because right now they are killing one another, and the battle is on! Our hearts lie in the balance. The world lies in the balance.

So what can we do? We can meditate with good intent. We can ponder a better world in unison, sending our wishes for a better place for our children to grow up in out into the universe. Our thoughts are energy. Energy makes up our reality. Our thoughts become reality. Everything in our reality was born of thought. It is a powerful process once it is begun.

Many people focusing on similar intent is a powerful energy in our universe.

That is how we came to be in this situation. The entire human race is expecting an apocalypse of one sort or another, and our thought is a powerful creator.

It comes with a measure of responsibility. Once you have the knowledge that reality is born of your thoughts, you become aware of the need to clean up your thought process. This is a hard task, because we are actually asking ourselves to undergo a real change. Not an exterior one that people perceive, while deep inside you are still thinking the same negative stuff.

A real change starts to happen. You begin to notice when the interior voice starts talking trash about the guy who just cut you off, and begin to see yourself as you go from lane to lane trying to get to work on time. You see that this is yourself, and gently correct the babble in your head. As this starts to happen, you begin to undergo real change, and your reality begins to change also.

The problems become not so much problems as mere challenges that will be overcome. It happens because you are reeling in those chaotic and angry thoughts that the lower self is broadcasting to the brain. All those little nagging urges, the cigarette addictions and alcohol and drug addictions, all are heeding the urges from their lower selves, and letting the lower self be your motivation. You begin to take control of the lower self and make your own decisions from a higher perspective.

When you begin to hear the higher self, the lower baser urges become less urgent, less of a necessity. Now you can begin to grow out of these addictions.

This sounds easy, but in reality a lot of people never get away from listening to their lower selves. People will pursue these addictions to their graves sometimes, never heeding the call of their higher spirit.

The inevitable growth process that begins with simple focus on the breath plants the seeds that make you start to look at these baser urges as the things that cause you to be depressed and unhappy and dissatisfied with everything and everyone.

Spending time in your own head with good intent will lead you to the realization that most of the time it is things you really don't need that you are unhappy about, and you move more and more towards that ideal as change manifests in your physical body from the chi you are taking in with that positive intent.

People with addictions can benefit very much from learning to control that lower self. Tell that voice to shut up and that YOU are in control and that you are not going to drink that day whether you are going to sleep that night or not.

When it comes to addiction to any substance, whether it be nicotine, or alcohol or drugs, you need to keep in mind that the entire society we live in is set up to encourage you to fail in your quest for sobriety. We go through life hearing, "I've been trying to quit smoking, but it is so hard to do!" Or "I would quit drinking, but life sucks and it is the only thing that helps me feel better."

Well if you really want to quit you have to man up and not cop out at the first rough patch that comes your way. This entire society tells you it is ok to fail, you can always try again.

Well if you really want to change then it is NOT ok to cop out and try again. There was once a time when if you gave up and didn't do what you had to do, you would starve to death.

The concept remains the same, with the same result. It simply takes longer than it used to so it seems so much more acceptable to us. The truth is that dying from your addiction is a terrible way to go. Your quality of life will improve dramatically by changing your behavior and putting that abuse to yourself behind you for good.

You have to be the one to make that decision, and then appeal to your higher self for help with that voice in your head that tells you that it is OK to indulge yourself one more time. Your lower self will kill you if you let it run your life as it has no self control and its influence is strong on the waking self. That little voice is hard to ignore, so you have to change what it is saying to you. This is possible if you ask yourself for help. Your higher self wants you to be happy and will help if you ask.

The experience of the drug addict or the alcoholic is not only their own. People around them see and experience this and learn from it. This too is the nature of things and a part of the wheel. Those people can see their pain and experience their own experience from this. Lessons are learned and the greater purpose served even still.

More on Meditation

So far I have described passive meditations that you perform seated or lying down. There are other forms of meditation that are more dynamic, and involve movement of the body in conjunction with controlled breathing that can be very effective for some of us that may have a problem with the more relaxed meditations.

Driving can be a form of dynamic meditation as you drive and listen to music or not. Even if you are listening to music you can spend time visualizing that energy flow around your chakras and breathing it in and out.

Walking also can be a great moving meditation. For those looking for something more advanced, there is Tai' Chi, Red Dragon Tai' chi, which involves a stick or staff, Aikido, Kuji-in, Chi Kung, or even the more martial arts like Kung Fu or Tai' Kwan Do involve a moving Kata or flowing series of movements that take total concentration and poise.

All of these will put you into a meditative state if you approach it with that intent. I walk every day for only ten to twenty minutes at a time, but I walk as fast as I can and practice yogic breathing as I walk, and circulate energy along my chakras as I walk. This is a great energy building exercise to help you in your practice.

The purpose of writing this book is indeed so that you as the reader may develop your own practice. It is my sincere hope that this book will stir the ancestral memory of even a handful of people and get them meditating with positive and healing intent. It is proven that meditation physically changes the brain. Meditating with healing or positive intent accelerates these changes.

Other changes are bound to occur with doing this work also. You will come to a point where taking in things that are not good for your spirit will become more difficult for you.

You will find that the positive effects from these things becomes harder and harder to achieve as the self knowledge grows and you see it as the self destructive behavior it really is. You will begin to change for the better. You will begin to become the more spiritual person you were meant to be.

The compulsion to do better will become so unbearable that you are forced into the crucible of change, to be annealed and melded into a better more well rounded person.

You will desire a balance, even if total abstinence is not achieved at first, the desire for it manifests in your brain somehow, and the seeds of change sprout and begin to manifest.

You become a better person just from becoming conscious of the chi energy and how to focus your attention on your breath.

The meditations just augment the process, helping you to improve your focus and visualization skills. Eventually you will become more conscious of the chi energy, and begin to actually feel it and in some cases see it if you are one of the more visually attuned.

With these changes comes empathy for others and the world that is sometimes quite painful to deal with. You can improve your shielding abilities to some extent, but there will be times when you are walking through the world and be exposed to things in people that just hurt to be around.

Some people are very negative influences energetically speaking, and I have that quality myself if I am in a negative place in my own head.

This is something I am acutely aware of, and I feel from the other perspective how I am perceived, and it causes me great pain and shame when I am in an emotional state of mind and sometimes speak harshly or just growl at someone unexpectedly, as I feel their shock and fear and see that look of unease come over them.

Yes fear. I am a bigger than life guy, and I don't realize what a gorilla I can appear to be to the average person. Whereas I see myself just grumping and being gruff, they see this strong guy who looks capable of harming them.

The Black Dog

Short of someone trying to hurt me or my family I would never see a reason to be violent in this world. I believe one of the biggest sins you can commit is to keep someone from experiencing this life, good and bad. However, I am going to do everything in my power to keep on experiencing my own experience, and I intend to see to it that my family does too, and I see no wrong in that.

Battling my way to this conclusion was a part of my growth process. I no longer felt like I should take a life, even in defense of my own. I could not bring myself to make this decision for my family, and I knew that I was honor bound to defend them regardless of my spiritual leanings. So I held on to a part of my warrior self, to keep put away inside me like a weapon I could pull out of my pocket at will. There is a time and place for that too, as it is all a part of the wheel.

This part of me started acting out when the Kundalini energy started coming up in me. I went into a near psychotic depression as I was forced to deal with this warrior side of myself and feel at the same time how it affects others. It hurt, and I knew it.

I suddenly realized that everything I do is hurting my spirit, and the spirits of those around me, and that I had to do more to change my whole outlook on life.

I felt guilt, for all the years of abuse to myself. It beat me up to the point that I was seriously thinking I had lost my mind, or that I was going to have a nervous breakdown, when the clouds suddenly cleared away, and light came back to me again. I felt like I had re-emerged from the darkness having been annealed and strengthened spiritually.

I feel a light within myself that is demanding deep spiritual change, and it is drawing me towards the love and light.

The Awakening of the Kundalini energy is a powerful thing, and has resulted in psychotic breaks in people when they were not fundamentally ready for it. By that statement, I mean you have to get your spiritual house in order.

I don't think I was quite ready for it when it happened to me, and I thought I was having a psychotic break with reality as this unbelievable rush of peace/love/joy overtook me. However, I could not bring myself to go to the doctor for it as it did not seem to be something I wanted or needed to medicate away.

I became filled with energy, and I am sure some people thought that I was on drugs of one sort or another, when in reality I was undergoing a powerful transformation.

I went home and danced for the first time in my life, as I had always been too "cool" to dance and look silly. Suddenly I was unable to stop myself, and I danced with my wife till 3-4 in the morning for three weeks straight as I was making up for lost time and had to deal with this energy coursing through me.

For most people this phenomenon does not last for more than a couple days to a couple of weeks. I kept waiting for this feeling to leave me and the inevitable crash that would come, but it never really left.

Now I find that I am riding on this energy high most of the time. On the flip side I find that when I am in a low spot that my sadness can be overwhelming. However my low spots never last long anymore and are much easier to deal with as I can now recognize the motivations for them for what they are, petty and self serving most of the time.

Through this process, with the meditation practice and focus on the space within, you will examine yourself in detail. You already know what you have to change about yourself. For me it is the very way I think. I present myself as a kind and gentle person, but people can sense the warrior spirit within me and react with fear if I am angry and this anger and fear is what I need to eliminate from my life.

When I manage to permanently quiet the angry voice in my head, I will be more in balance with my spiritual ideal.

Some thoughts on the 2012 phenomenon

As 2012 rolls on, we are 11 months in, and I am certain that there are others out there like me who are attempting to tie up their loose ends so to speak. Many things are culminating that could and will result in major changes in the world. There is a change in the paradigm coming and how you approach it will make a lot of difference in the outcome.

As tensions rise with the growing prices for all the basic necessities that the average person needs to live day to day, the way you deal with other people's negativity will make a big difference in how hard this transition is.

There is enough of this tension and stress energy in the world right now that if you are any kind of an empath and feel for your fellow man, things are getting harder and harder to be around. So many people are hurting you can find yourself withdrawing from the world, when instead what we need to be doing is reaching out and offering support to those who are hurting and that need it.

Just helping one person to feel better or filling some need for a person who has no other way of getting that particular thing goes ever so much farther than you may realize. It can move the world.

Paying it forward in some small way is all it takes, because there are a lot of us who are not as bad off as some of the rest. You know every time you pay it forward there is a chance that it will come back, if not to you, then maybe to the next person who needs it.

We are living in some interesting times as I said, and those of you who are paying attention may be wondering as I am if we really are living in the end times. I think it may be near the end of the current paradigm, but what way it is going to go has yet to materialize.

I truly believe that the way this is going to go has a lot to do with the level that we are able to connect as a species on this planet and lose the lines we create between ourselves over color and idealism.

The human race is all one species, and more and more people are waking up to that fact and realizing that we all need to change to make it all work.

Overpopulation will become a problem very soon on this planet and Water and food will become the sought after commodities. A lot of people think they can simply go to the woods and hunt and fish to feed their families, but in a real world situation that person is going to find that there a lot of other hungry people with the same idea, and game will soon be in short supply.

Civil war and violence will soon follow, and I am no prophet, I am just watching the trends, and watching the tension grow as the powers that be are for some reason polarizing this country into a place that is hard to recognize as the USA I grew up in.

You can prepare the best you can and that is the best you can do. Preparing your spirit to deal with this diversity will go a long ways towards your long term survival. Finding the peace that meditation provides is a great release when it is all too much to think about.

Every piece of adversity we encounter is a test. How you react to these circumstances educates our collective consciousness. If you choose to react with indifference when you see a person in pain, the entire world suffers from that small indifference.

If instead, you stand up and fill that need for that person, with no expectation in return, again, the whole world reacts to the positive. Every single time you are repulsed by the negative images that surround you in this world, the entire collective consciousness registers and remembers that in the akashic memory.

Every time you react with compassion to others needs, you are educating your own reality to react with compassion to your own. Paying it forward has never been more important.

Grab your brother by the hand and help him up too, for we are our brother's keeper, as we are all one when you remove the separation that living the human experience enforces on us.

The notion that we are all living separate lives is an illusion. We all breathe the same air and partake of the same nourishment and water. We all need these things as children of the mother Earth. All we are is animated stardust held together with this thinly veiled illusion of our minute to minute reality, but we all need these things, water, air and food/fuel.

We have to keep the energy burning and keep the knowledge evolving until we finally either kill one another off or learn to live with one another. I choose to live... What is your choice?

Until we realize that what effect's the Gulf of Mexico has a direct effect on what happens in Northern Europe, and by default the entire ocean, and the same goes for the pacific loop current that connects Alaska, Canada, and north America directly to the nuclear disaster in Fukushima Japan, then we are going to be divided into these races and keep ourselves segregated.

Together as one we can pay it forward to the needy among us. We can support our elders and make everyone healthy and happy.

When we realize that we are all working towards the same goal of helping this world support us, we will be approaching the right mind set. There is a growing movement out there that is educating the rest as best they can.

Bombs will not soothe it. Guns will not make it better. The wounds need the salve of love. If the price of just a few of these bombs was spent to feed and house hungry people, think of the difference it could make for the needy ones.

Maybe with a little nourishment we can grow this into the sort of unity that we all need to survive and flourish as a species, devoid of the separation of race and creed.

We are blessed with the knowledge of the ancients at the touch of a mouse pad. Yet we wander ignorantly and aimlessly because seeking this knowledge has been beat down in us until we can hardly believe in a world of magic anymore.

Well, the magic is still there. It is right in your hands, and it is just waiting for you to realize it is there for you. It is there for the healing and power you need to get through this life.

All you have to do is go after it and practice some simple concepts and take the steps that your mind will show you.

Once you open yourself to the fact that the world is not all as it seems on the surface, it can awaken an interest in you that will drive you down this spiritual path like an engine.

More and more knowledge comes to your fingertips. You can use your intuition to ferret out the teachers in your world. When you are ready, they will come.

Charlatans and fakers will come with them. You can usually tell them by the high price tag attached with their learning. If a teacher wants a financial commitment from you more than it costs him to facilitate the teaching you are probably not in the right place.

This knowledge has always been there for the true seeker, and it should not involve signing a contract or giving your bank account information to achieve a better reality. All that it takes is a little bit of focus and commitment to change the way you think.

Preppers

Now that it is 2012 and the epitome that we are all materializing is finally becoming our reality many people are in a mode of preparation. They think, "I will do this" and "I will do that" if everything goes to hell in a hand basket. The reality will be very different from what they think.

People in general in the world follow the trends, and they may think they are prepared with some food put back and maybe a bug out bag ready so they can go out in the woods and hunt game and survive and think they are as prepared as they need to be.

The reality will be ruled by the grocery store supply chain. As soon as this chain is disrupted all hell is going to break loose.

The inner cities are three days from total chaos at any given time. If the grocery stores ran out of staples, the people would revert to the strong shall survive within short order.

Those that take to the woods will find a lot of other people thinking the same thing and shooting at anything that moves, as game will become scarce very quickly with so many hungry humans with firearms storm the woods in search of meat shooting anything that moves.

The value of the human life will go down exponentially, and we will kill one another off until the supply matches the demand once again.

You need to look at food sources closer to you. If worse came to worse there is a lot of large anthills in my yard 3-4 ft. tall with a lot of ants in them. Good renewable protein source. We have lots of rabbits here and I got a lot of .22 shells, so I could eat them from time to time, lots of birds, my grandfather cooked crow and pigeon and called it "squab" and it wasn't bad at all.

Frogs, snakes, and even slugs and snails and grubs are all good protein sources if you are truly hungry, the animal in you will come out sooner or later, and the sooner the better.

Right now the information is available at your fingertips to see how to process and prepare meats and game. Never before has it been there for you to read about, but instead was passed down with word of mouth and direct hands on experience.

Life is messy

That hand's on experience is missing from the latest generations, and that is no insult with all the knowledge available to them. It is all there to look up so why go through the mess of getting your fingers bloody to learn how to do it, right?

The same can be said of human relationships in the current paradigm. Everyone is attached to their hand held devices, with any whim available with a few keystrokes. Why have friends that have needs and messes that don't involve you when you can read all about it online?

Well it takes a little getting your hands wet to learn the intricacies of interpersonal relationships or preparing your own venison stew. You have to get messy to eat, and even if someone else is cleaning up the mess, you are responsible for it also whether you slaughtered that animal or not.

It's messy, and you are a part of it all, and other people have to eat too, so share the bounty and pay it forward if you have something from the struggle to share.

The struggle to survive is becoming harder every day as prices rise on even the basic necessities. With the loss of value on most of the world's currencies, inflation will inevitably go out of control. Already we are looking at almost $5.00 a gallon of gas here this summer.

Milk is coming up on $4.00 a gallon. Bread $3.00 a loaf and up. A pack of Toilet Paper is ten bucks. These necessities are adding up. Wages are not rising to follow suit and the gap is widening.

I foresee families having to consolidate and throw in together to have enough people working to cover a households needs, and we are already needing more space.

If the infrastructure can keep functioning and people can keep working through the recession that is looming ahead they are going to have to get used to some changes in their mindsets. Population control will become a mainstream topic as the world struggles with an ever growing population and a dwindling food supply that has been polluted with genetically modified freak plants that will be much harder to weed out than they were to introduce.

The ramifications from the ecological atrocities that occurred in the last few years have yet to fully materialize. The bottom of the gulf remains smothered in tons upon tons of heavy oil that is not going to go away and will be mucking up the environment for years to come.

The reactors of Fukushima are still filling the air and seas with radiation, with no solution or end to it in sight.

At this point in time regardless of what happens with the culmination of 2012, our entire way of life is on the brink of a huge change. The American dream will be a thing of the past.

We in the US have been spoiled by easy times and a stability that people in other parts of the world have never experienced. Regardless of what some people think, there are no promises that will keep it as it is. It takes the support of the people to make a country or a city or even a home work.

People have to get up and do the essential functions that keep the home, city, or country running. Certain things have to be observed and done.

A budget must be arrived at and adhered to or else it will fail. Food must be acquired or grown or it will fail. Water has to be there to drink and to clean, or it will fail. If sanitation is not kept up anything will sicken and die, and it will fail. Like a simple houseplant, we all need the special things that enable us to live.

At this point in time it seems to me "we" as a species have failed miserably, and we seem to be as a plague on this planet. A visitor from another world may come in someplace clean, and be marveling over the beautiful blue oceans, then the palm trees and rugged mountains, and huge forests of pine and fir.

Then suddenly they come across a great place where the earth has been covered by the hard scab of concrete, while the vapors of our industrial pollution come up like the steam from fresh excrement in the snow, and they may think we are as a cancer on this planet. A great wound to be cleansed for the good of all.

I would not be the least surprised if the great mother shrugged us all into the sea, because people, we deserve no better. We have abused the beautiful home we have been given, and it is almost beyond saving for our grandchildren. Right now some of you are thinking, "Not Me! I recycle!" or "I keep my house clean!"

Choices

It is much bigger than all that. The choices we make every day, with every penny we spend and every time we interact with another living being, are choices we make that are changing our world every second.

Every time you buy locally grown produce instead of the supermarket Produce that may be weeks old you are benefitting the people in your local community. You are benefitting yourself too as the weeks old vegetables from the big chain store are drained of vital energy. It wasn't raised where you live to help you fend off the allergens in the area that you live in.

The produce from your local farmers market is much closer to the living plant than stuff you will get in a store and has so much more chi or life energy in it than the store bought stuff that comes from thousands of miles away from you. Instead of weeks from the earth it is days. The difference in health benefits is dramatic.

If you buy your meat from a local butcher shop you are keeping the money in the people's hands instead of putting it in the deep pockets of the industrial machine that is the modern food supply in this world we live in.

Every time you react with kindness even if you are unhappy, you are adding a drop of love to this angry and impatient world we are experiencing and manifesting all the time. When you turn off the television and pick up a musical instrument, or sing, or whistle, or just sit quietly and meditate, you are for that time not adding to the symphony of destruction that we call entertainment today.

Imagine if our thoughts do create what we experience, what the effect of a single violent film, compared to say spending a couple hrs laughing as you and your child play a game together. The difference is profound in the change of focus and how that affects everything. How you think teaches the collective consciousness to create what we experience as a whole all the time we are living it.

Anyone who is not seeking change is supporting the current paradigm of destruction and endless labor to support a life you barely get to live, spending the majority of it working so you must be away from it to pay the beast that is our current reality. It is killing us all and it has to change.

You work every day of your life, day in and day out and the carrot on the end of your stick is that you may have a home paid off and be able to retire to it and live in peace in your elder years.

The reality is that you never own that piece of land you are living on, and if you don't keep paying the beast his taxes, they will come and remove you from your property despite the fact that you worked your entire life away for it.

Still we keep paying in and supporting this system. The paradigm has to change and we all have to do it together. People as a species need to realize that life goes on beyond the next half hour, and think more about the world that the next generations will grow up in and get our act together now before we do something we can't fix.

Realization

The only way to stop the madness that is the world we are living in is to change the way we think. To do that you first have to REALIZE that you need to. Then after you have your moment of realization, you must remember, and start to focus your mind on the love and peace that is inside of us all.

I don't know if the meditation causes Kundalini to begin, or the visualization of energy movement around the chakras causes it, or the combination of the two, but I feel very strongly that meditating with healing intent is a tool that helps you to keep your focus on the positive aspect of our lives, and the healing is love, realized. These three things combined is a very strong trinity.

Sometimes the healing that is needed is your own. You may find it hard to focus on anything other than your own pain. This can be the most difficult healing of all, the healing of your own spirit.

People in this world do irresponsible and sometimes thoughtless things to one another every day of our lives. Sometimes the things done are terrible things that are very hard to get past. You may have done something that you feel you can't forgive yourself or someone else for. You may think your soul is too broken to fix. You may be affected by all of the above.

The reality is that you have to forgive. That is not saying that what happened is acceptable. What you are doing is taking back the energy you lose by giving thought to this act or moment, by consciously severing the energy connection to that moment.

You are connected to everything you can realize in your consciousness, including the terrible things that happen to us all.

You can sever that connection with the same realization. Your thoughts make your reality. How you think is how you respond to the moment of realization.

A better reaction can be trained into your consciousness. We don't have to react the way we have been conditioned. We can choose how we are going to react to these terrible thoughts that all of us entertain. They are a terrible drain on our life force energy or chi.

Once you start to realize more often that your bad reaction is not appropriate, you will have begun to change the thought process and guide it back to a more centered state, where you can have the peace and love you so much need and deserve.

Forgiving is not about saying, "That's OK" It is about reclaiming the energy you lose by remembering these unfortunate moments in all of our lives.

Once you begin to recapitulate or recall this energy, you will find yourself being more positive as you have more energy to devote to the reality you are creating. Just starting to heal those pains will make a positive improvement in your life, and by default it will get better.

I am not saying that all the sudden your life will become a bed of roses, but examining these events that drain your energy thoroughly and with an honest eye during your healing meditations can lessen the impact of the burden you carry, similar to how familiarity with something you are afraid of will lessen the connection to the fear response, and by default you will be less afraid. You will have healed that fear response through a conscious act to do so.

The same as forgiving a grievous act that was perpetrated on you can be lessened with familiarity with that memory. Don't forget to consciously cut that connection every time this unwanted concept comes into your mind.

I use a mental sword with a keen edge that can cut through any connection. My wife uses a big pair of mental scissors and snips it to cut the ties. This can also be accomplished by writing the thoughts down on a piece of paper and then burning or destroying it.

The thought process is supported by the physical act. It serves the same purpose as a ritual or placebo. It is performing an action with a specific intent to create a reaction, and it works a little better every time you do it. Your mind becomes trained to react differently. You can change your world with the power of your thoughts. It really is just that simple! You have the ability to choose something better.

Forgiving can be the hardest part of the growth process, and the most limiting part of who you are. If you can learn to forgive the negative things done to you, you can grow and become more than the person that was effected by these negative things.

You can in effect choose to feel different about the things that have damaged you to the point that you are no longer damaged, but instead are annealed into a harder and more resilient spirit.

Steel is strong, but if it is beaten long and hard, it anneals into stronger steel as the molecules change their position and become aligned with one another. The pain of the beating makes it stronger.

You too can become annealed by the beatings this reality deals out to you, and in fact you can grow beyond them and transcend into the spiritual and loving creature you are meant to be.

Starting over

Nobody can keep you where you are right now but yourself! YOU are the limiting factor here, not the world around you or the circumstances you are in. You can build an entirely new identity from the foundation you have already created. Don't let someone abuse you, because we all have the power to stand on our own regardless of what anyone else tells you. Don't let anything stand in your way.

When I started writing this book I was 300 lbs and not happy about anything I had done in my life. With the new skills I acquired from the proper teacher, I was able to think beyond the box that I had created for myself. I began to see myself as more than I was before. I had my moment of realization, through the meditation I was doing daily. I realized I needed to make some changes, so I started with one.

I started doing pushups every day, and at first I could only do seven, but I kept at it. Within a week I was doing ten, and within a few months I was doing 30-50 a day. People started to notice in no time, and I started feeling better about myself with every comment, and I began to transform for the better. I did this devoting just one minute a day towards this goal. My intent delivered the results.

The positive comments kept me motivated, and within a year, I had dropped a hundred lbs and was still doing my pushups every day that I went to work and sometimes more. I added a daily ten minute walk to my routine and got even better results as my cardio vascular system responded to the short and easy exertions.

I walked and visualized the energy circulating through my chakras as I went, and made my walk a short moving meditation. I did this with patience, and kept at it whether it seemed to be effective or not.

Before I realized it had happened, I had transformed myself into something better with no more than 11 minutes a day invested in physical activity.

I think that combining the physical activity with the energy circulation visualization and meditation and focus on the positive aspects of the activities I was doing combined to make it all much more effective.

Seeing this positive effect was empowering for me. I realized that I had effected a change in the better for myself. Now I feel like a kid again, bursting with Chi that has to be dealt with daily or I think I would lose my mind.

Realizing all that I had done had really paid off, I decided to pick another positive thing to add to my routine. Music was a natural choice as I had played guitar since I was a young kid and never really learned because I was lazy. I decided to pick up the guitar every day and see if I could improve on that.

Now a few months later, I can play along with anything on the radio as it comes at me, even if not note for note, I can sound like I am part of the rhythm section at least. Once again a few minutes a day were sacrificed for this endeavor, and my positive intent produced results.

I am a much more left brained person than I used to be and even my art is more abstract than it was before.

The Power of Cumulative effects

I believe why a lot of people say they can't do this or can't do that is because they may go through the motions for a few days, and when they get no results from their actions they stop trying.

It takes a lot more than a few days. It takes setting a pattern of positive activity every day until your psyche embraces that activity and starts to fall into line with it and give you those elusive results.

You have to train your brain, the same as when you start to meditate, at first you seem scattered and unfocused, but do it for a year and you will have had a dramatic change in perception. The cumulative effect is undeniable.

Do pushups for a year, and instead of doing the 7-10 you will start out with, by the end of the year you will have done thousands of pushups, and that has a cumulative result from spending that one minute a day.

I think this is why people fail in so many endeavors of self improvement. The lack of follow through is built into us by the sedentary lifestyle that is the modern age. Our brain is used to quick distractions provided by all of the electronic devices that we all use as part of the modern society.

The thing is, you don't have to jump up and start right into a 30 minute workout. That may burn you out if you have been sedentary for a long period of time. The object is not to hurt yourself, the object is to move a little bit and encourage your energy to begin to grow.

Real change takes time as you go through the evolutionary process. You may not see it day to day, but over a year, the cumulative impact is huge, and others will see a dramatic change for that little effort. You may think I don't have time for this, but it starts with one minute. We all have a minute.

We all have YEARS to fill. We have to start thinking longer term than the next half hour of immediate gratification. We all want that candy bar after lunch every day, but would you feed your dog a jumbo Hershey bar with almonds and ten cups of coffee every day?

Of course you wouldn't, but that is just what we do to ourselves! We treat ourselves worse than our dogs, and wonder why we are unhealthy. If you take a realistic look, it will become obvious what the problems are, and by meditating, you will begin to examine those problem areas until the desire to stop perpetuating those problems begins to take form. The idea will grow and grow until you have to act on it.

That crucible of change will have begun with or without you even being aware of it.

If we sit around and constantly think thoughts of the negative, while we sit in front of the television or computer and are bombarded with messages of inadequacy, "Is your belly fat bothering you?" "Going bald?" "Is your penis too small, or won't stand up for you?" The list goes on and on and the litany of woes is endless.

These commercials program inadequacy into your thoughts and keep you focused on how you look, or what people think about what you wear, and it is all to program your mind to spend money on useless products, or products with so many side effects that taking them for the minor benefit they give you seems silly if you really weigh the pros and cons.

Sometimes it can seem overwhelming, but instead of taking some chemical to boost your metabolism, just try to eat more things that are straight from the earth to you. The chi or life force is more present than it is in processed foods. As soon as you start eating healthier, your whole body responds as it soaks up the nutrients like a sponge.

You can still eat what you want, just try to eat healthy more often than not and your body will respond in kind. Tip the balance back towards the positive and stop the downward spiral that half this country seems to be in today.

Once again you have to train your mind to think of ways to make a positive impact on your own life instead of settling for constant deterioration we have been programmed to believe is the only life we can have. We can have a better life without a whole lot of effort.

It starts with one minute focusing on something positive. Anything can blossom from that point that you can imagine. Every time you make a positive step you become better as a whole and everyone around you benefits by osmosis, the same as everyone around you suffers from the negativity.

Depression

Focusing on the negative things is a very hard thing to get away from in this world. That is why training your mind into a more positive place is so badly needed. Depression robs you of vital energy and leaves you with nothing left to give back to the world.

If you are not a gregarious person and find yourself believing you are alone in the world. Consider putting a birdfeeder outside of a window where you can sit and watch this instead of the television. Soon a lot of birds will become frequent visitors, and their songs can be a great comfort.

You will develop a relationship with these birds that is beneficial to you both. You will be supporting them through the harsh winters when food is scarce, and they will bring you up with their presence on those lonely days and give you something positive to focus on without the responsibility that having a dog or cat involves.

This can let you get into a positive place where you can do good things for yourself and others, and takes you away from that television or computer and away from the negative ads for at least that much time. Every little bit helps when you are trying to find some light in the world. You can choose to make it better one minute at a time.

You can choose to get outside and let the natural healing that comes from the earth and sun soak into you a little more, even if you just get out and walk around the house for a minute soaking up these natural energies can be a big pick me up.

Ask your higher self to help you to quiet that nagging little voice inside of all of us, and to tell it to say positive things instead of negative ones. Ask out loud, to fortify this request.

Your higher self is there listening, and can help with that voice inside. Your higher self wants to see you happy and more balanced so that you can shine that light on others.

It will help you to get there if you let it.

Life challenges us all and some more than others. You may find yourself or a loved one dealing with a life changing illness, or something else that rocks your world. It happens to all of us. You have to step up and deal with that, all the way to the end if necessary. All of us do.

I have come to the realization that we have to experience these things so that we can experience the positive and see the contrast. The yin and the yang are to be found in everything we see. If it were not for darkness we would not recognize the light. If it were not for hatred we would not recognize love.

Pain can be one of the purest emotions, and once the contrast is recognized, one can start to strive to rebalance the yin and the yang, and to recognize the small beauty to be had in many things all around us, even as the world is seemingly in turmoil.

You have to appreciate seeing the glitter of the sun on the ice, and the way the trees look when the sun is going down and only the very tops are still lit up. You have to see the beautiful yellow that is the dandelion some consider a weed.

The Iridescence of that oily mud puddle shows you all of God's colors and reflects them back for you to take in and realize.

A wooly caterpillar crawling on a leaf demonstrates the complexity and metamorphosis that we can all achieve when we realize we are truly spiritual creatures in this body for only a short time before we are again released back to the collective as the intelligent energy that we are.

Dealing with my own inner demons has almost killed me in the past, so one has to find a way through the depression that comes from dwelling in the lower self. Music has just about saved my life I think.

If you listen, there is a higher voice inside you that you can tune in to. It will guide you through the darkness if you let it be your guide instead of the lower self.

The lower self is the source of those urges that seem so important that if you don't fill them you will crumble and become ineffective. You have a higher self that can tune that inner voice right up so that it becomes supportive instead of negative.

It is a choice that you have to consciously make often enough that it becomes unconscious. Know thyself and all in moderation is more than a Gnostic catch phrase.

If depression in any form is affecting your ability to function, you have to find a way through it all. Use that negative energy as a driver to become a better person and cut the energy connections to that place that you seem so stuck in. It can change. You can grow and adapt and over time deal with it for what it is, simply a temporary change in perspective.

Our time here is to evolve, not to stay the same stuck in some proverbial rut that we think ourselves unable to get out of. We can effect change a lot easier than we have been brought up to believe. We are not destined to die having made no impact on this world.

We have a job to do here and our job is to steward the world and ourselves, and to do that we have to get proactive and start to grow as a species. The current way is not going to be able to be sustained.

It is very obvious that the current reality is undergoing some massive changes. To me it looks like the Mayan's may have been on to something as we wind up to some sort of cataclysmic event. We all need to be very adaptable right now as this world is in flux and we are caught up in it all.

Some parts of the world like Japan and Indonesia have already experienced their cataclysm, and are now living in the aftermath. We are a hairs breadth away from nuclear war as Israel and Iran posture towards war with the US, China and Russia watching tensely in the background.

Now is the time to make these positive changes. We must get our proverbial acts together and get the right things happening to circumvent this cataclysm. I believe we can make it easier or harder depending on what paradigm we are envisioning and focusing our attention on.

Somewhere in your genetic code or ancestral spirit you know that these things are true. It is time that we all begin to really evolve as a species and take control of our destinies as the stewards of the beautiful world and incredible bodies we were blessed with.

We can become anything we want to and it is time to become better so that our grandchildren have the same bounties that we enjoy. They deserve better than we are giving them now and so do we.

The time is now. Only you can change your life. You need to stop waiting for someone else to do it for you. You are your own dog and you need to ask yourself where are you going to be next year? Five years down the road?

Are you going to still be having the same problems you have now, or are you going to get proactive and get yourself fixed so that you can be of benefit to this world and influence everything in it for the better?

It all begins with a thought. Realize that you don't have to be what you have been told you are. We all have the ability to learn and grow and to become a different creature than the one that we started out as.

Human beings have the ability to program yourself by the power of your thoughts and you can learn to become happy by taking that first step towards something positive.

If that little voice in your head tells you otherwise, look to your higher self for help and guidance to help you find the answers we all so badly need. That little voice in your head can become your friend instead of your detractor.

I don't want to give the impression that my thoughts are all lilacs and roses. I am still working to train my thoughts towards the positive, but as I have done so, it has become glaringly obvious that everything is getting better even as I write.

It is all in my reaction to the pain and the love that comes my way. You have to be grateful for it all. You have to grow through it all. That is what makes it all matter.

There will always be hard times, and there will be times when healing can't happen and that person's package is so damaged that to prolong the pain by performing healing would be detrimental. This is something you will have to arrive at through personal choice and individual experience.

Hopefully when these hard decisions come to you, your higher self will guide you to make the right decision as to whether to heal this person or not.

We are not God, and the final decision rests with the creator. We are all here for just a fleeting time, and our lives are like the seasons of the year and gone just as fast. All of us dogs have our day, and there is no avoiding that no matter how you can heal.

If however you have a chance to do healing for someone, believe with all your heart that it can be done, because we are all indeed creatures of spirit and intelligent energy. As such we can create with the power of the thoughts we think. You can choose to be more than you are, but the choice has to be made, and steps taken to become that.

No matter what, that person realizes that another soul cared enough to focus on their well being for the duration, and that can be a beautiful placebo to fortify natural healing. It is all good for the soul of the healer and the person being healed. Comfort is to be had on both ends of the equation.

It doesn't come for free. The steps have to be taken for the forward progress to happen. Every single one of us is capable of becoming that more spiritual and involved person that we are meant to be. We are a part of it all and we need to be making the progress as a people to bridge the gap of racism, or culturalism, or religions, and become fellow humans and take care of one another as such. We are our brother's keeper.

Universal truth

God is way too big for one little religion. We all need to face the fact that there is a universal truth in all religion that is based on love and belief so that we can all realize that all of our individual paths to our God source are valid. We all have a right to believe in anything that harms nobody, and that causes nobody to be persecuted for their believing differently.

If you find yourself sitting in judgment of my beliefs, well I completely understand as most of this country is pretty earthbound in their thinking and concepts such as chi are not yet in the textbooks.

If you have been reading this and feel that you don't believe what I believe, that is all ok too. We all have a right to think any way we want to, and skepticism is appreciated. At least you were distracted from the mayhem for a moment.

I am just trying to share what I have learned through a lot of exploration into myself and the history of people who have done the same. If you can get past the self serving sludge that makes up most of our daily thoughts you can do anything. You have to believe you can.

Then do it... just like that. Move beyond it all.

Your tomorrow can be different than today. We must all embrace one another as brother and sisters in one big human family. Muslims, Buddhists, Christians and Catholics can live in harmony with Native Americans and other indigenous people and their belief systems. All that is needed is for us all to see we are all related. A'ho! Mitakuye' O'yasin!

We all depend on one another for the goods that we need to get by from day to day. Now is the time to develop relationships with neighbors and figure out your niche in the new world order, as it is truly coming about as I write this.

The time of separation is almost over, and I feel that soon we will be forced to depend on our neighbors and them on us to watch out for one another in this time of change.

Do you have something to offer in trade for the goods you need? Do you have a skill that is marketable? The time is now to learn one or two. We all tend to go different directions, and end up in different places due to the variability of our different perspectives. This helps fill many such niches for one another.

You need to find your own passion and learn it now so you know it when you need it to rely on. If you are passionate about what you do it will work out for you one way or another if you keep after it.

All the knowledge is there at your finger tips, so start digging and find yourself. You might find you are a much more talented individual than you thought yourself to be.

No matter what way you apply yourself just get started and do it. You will be doing yourself and everyone around you a favor when you do, because you will grow with every new exposure. It will all change your perspective into something better.

Somehow with all this information available to us we have lost sight of the wheel. It all goes around and keeps on going. Our children need a place on it and so do their children. It has to all go on, and we have to leave a usable planet for them to live on too. It's not ALL about us. It is about ALL of us.

The mainstream people now are thinking so short term and are so sure that everything will remain as it is. They think that we will always enjoy the luxuries we have right now. We have to take a longer term view on things. The cumulative effect is ever so much more important than the effects of the now.

Things you may not notice much now can have a terrible effect on you long term, and you have to take steps towards the positive or else you will indeed suffer those effects in the long run. Life is hard on those who live in their lower selves.

I suffer with that myself, as I like to drink hard alcohol from time to time and I know it can kill me in time, and is doing me no good at all. However I still drink from time to time, and very much enjoy it when I do. Like I said I am working on it and indulging less and less, and I am pretty certain there will come a time when I just quit.

I recognize the self destructive nature of it, and it is one of the few things that nag at my soul. This is not a confession so much as I just didn't want anyone to feel that you cannot become better, regardless of our flaws. I also didn't want to mislead anyone into thinking I am better than anyone of you reading this. Life is a learning experience and I am learning right along with the rest of you.

We all suffer from our lower selves and deal with it the best we can. Surviving and growing is the key, and knowing you can be better every single day.

The time we spend away from our family is as important as the time we spend with it. The world you come in contact with when you are out there is your extended family. We all have to take care of one another and help back one another up against the rest of the world. We don't need universal healthcare for that, we just have to reach out and help one another. Problem solved.

There will come a time in all of our lives when we need help. I suggest you pay it forward so that when it is your time of need, there are people out there that you have helped. The time to pay it forward is now.

It seems funny how the harder you try the more gets heaped onto you. Life gets in the way of a spiritual mindset. Things happen all the time in life and largely life is a series of mishaps that you learn from, if you survive. Sometimes we get to be better people out of the deal if we get beat up long enough to learn to avoid it.

The weight of words

Our words have weight and can hurt more than a punch and inflict much more damage. A casual word spoken in frustration or anger can ruin relationships or end a life. It can wreck a career. You can influence others to take action that they normally would not have taken with just a casual word that you didn't give a second thought to.

All of this with the wrong words at the wrong time. Rash moves are best slept on overnight. They can often be seen for such by the light of the next day.

Many lives are ruined for not taking the time to reflect on a decision before action is taken. Bad moves are made in an instant and cannot be recalled like a chess game.

We have to walk carefully through this world and be conscious of the souls around us who are also trying to learn their way. All of us have had our moments on both sides of the yin and the yang

Life is such a delicate balancing act, and God help those who can't juggle at the same time! Following the right path is like balancing a pencil on your finger for the rest of your life. It may fall from time to time. Just pick it up and start again.

It is HARD to keep in line, and we are all fallible. It is a fine line we all walk between the light and the dark. However, most of us seem to balance it all out, and fall on one side or the other. I am trying to feed that white dog in my heart. What do YOU choose?

Working on depression

Here are some things that work to bring me out of the times my mindset gets caught up in the negative and I find myself desperate for anything to change it.

Music has to be the number one thing that gets me out of myself when I am in a low place. My music can make me forget about my problems for at least a while. Music can be therapeutic for joy or a bad day. Sometimes you feel like "don't worry, be happy", and sometimes it feels like "Just one of those days" Both serve their place and sooth the wounds the world puts on me.

Remember the line "Dance like nobody is looking?" Do that often and loudly. It doesn't matter how you are built you can use the music to get outside of yourself.

Just start with simple movements swaying to the music, and then gradually work in moving every part of your body. The energy will start to flow and your joints will be working. Smile as you dance, the whole point is to feel good and enjoy a little of your time in this world.

Add a hug to your greetings! It will bring a lot of warmth to your life, and the habit spreads. I will hug anyone and take all I can get. The warmth of a good hug can keep me going all day, and it is very therapeutic for just about anything ailing you.

This simple human contact may be the first time that person has been close to another human for a long time. They will appreciate it and reciprocate with a big smile. It lets someone know you really care if they live or die.

Hugs bring your heart energies together so you can feel that interaction even better through the heart chakras. We need that interaction on a spiritual level. Simple affection can be such a beautiful thing.

I try to hug my wife as often as I can, and it really helps me get through my day even if she just texts the word "HUGS" to me when we are apart.

I hug my friends too though, and even if some of them were a little stiff about it at first, they got with the program pretty soon, and now I rarely go anywhere and leave without a hug.

If I wake up on the wrong side of the bed so to speak, or just am not feeling that great, I am not above lying to myself to pick myself up. When a friend says, "How are you doing today?" I almost invariably answer back with "Excellent!" or "Fantastic!" No matter that my shoulder is killing me or that I got a headache from staying up too late playing music the night before.

After a while the answer becomes true as you realize that you really are good. No matter the aches and pains that I have I can still get up and do a few pushups and walk around. There are people so much worse in the world. It's a simple choice you can make to improve your attitude and how you respond to the world. It becomes habitual just like the negativity.

The habit of negativity is drilled into us by the materialistic world we live in. We have to change our mindsets to effect the real change we seek. A better reaction to how the world makes you feel can be built in with a few simple actions and reactions. These are small steps that can gradually help you to think better of yourself and the world around you.

You might not be able to get into heaven through acts, but positive actions can definitely give you a more positive self image.

My wife's brother recently passed away. He was one of those special souls that made you notice things. I didn't realize how much I would miss him, but now I try to spot the things He would have pointed out to me.

Some folks would have said he killed himself with alcohol, I tend to think he just enjoyed this life right to the end and did what he wanted, but along the way he touched a lot of hearts. I think he wanted to live right up to 2012, and made it to May. RIP Brother.

Anyhow, he made us notice the little things. He would point out that single ray of sunlight coming thru the shade that shined just so on the crystal jewel my wife had hung from the ceiling and how it splashed light over half the room.

He noticed how pretty the chamomile on the front hill smelled when I mowed the weeds out there. He had a way of pointing out the sublime stuff around you all the time and it was a beautiful thing. The world is lesser one beautiful and resilient old soul.

It is the mindset to look for. You have to appreciate the little things and the free things when times are hard and there is no light to be found. This can make a profound difference in the way you see things.

It started a couple years ago, me thinking I should get some of this down in writing. So I am taking the time to record my thoughts on the whole big picture as I see it. Are you holding on to anything that you need to record for future generations to learn or remember?

It is important right now to get that down and record your thoughts so that the living can take in the nourishment of your knowledge as well as the collective consciousness does when you die.

The fact that you are reading is a good sign. You are seeking change, or you would have dropped this book at the first biblical reference and gone on with your cynical self. I know there was a time I would have. Like I said earlier I think there is a universal truth in all religion.

Reincarnation

I happen to be slanted towards reincarnation for this reason. Our oldest daughter when she was three asked mommy, "Do you remember when I was the mommy and you were the little girl?"

Mommy said, "No, tell me about it" as she fastened rain boots onto her little feet.

"I used to use a buttonhook", and made a deft motion for a three year old that mimicked very well buttoning an old fashioned pair of boots with a old fashioned buttonhook. "We have one in the closet, I will show you" she said.

She got up and ran to the living room closet and retrieved a latch hook from a latch hook rug making set that looked for every respect like an old fashioned buttonhook!

The wife and I were dumbfounded, and this was a growing point in our spirituality. There is a continuity to it all that transcends the ages. I believe our soul goes on. This is what we must recognize, and ask the ancestors to help us to restore the ancient knowledge.

The frequencies have got to be unleashed. There are tones that can rock the world. There was once a knowledge based on sound that can move mountains and build pyramids. This I know in my gut, and hold true as one of my core beliefs.

This will be discovered again, and hopefully we won't destroy ourselves with the knowledge as we have in the past.

Colors are frequencies, music is frequencies, our reality is entirely built on the frequencies we can perceive the differences and work with them as a positive or negative force depending on the dog we are feeding the most.

If you are grooving all is good if you are warlike, you can work on your perspective if you choose, because something better is out there for you. Anger is not music but even heavy music can sound good when you are in a positive place. You have to apply it so.

The white or the black will prevail. Let us make this epitome an epitome of healing! Let the white and the light prevail to make our entire reality a better place for ALL of us. We can all be that more spiritual creature that the new paradigm will need. We can do this as easily as the opposite. The choice is yours...NOW. Choose, life or death, it really is that simple. Black and white, we are all those two dogs...

We will continue as two paradigms, motivated one against the other until the black and the white become one big gray area. Eventually one will rise above, and I hope we can manifest peace, because we all deserve it. We all deserve to simply relax and believe we have a right to exist. All of us, Just as we are.

Nobody can tell you yes or no. You have to decide these parameters on your own from your own experience. If anything I have said does not resonate with you, then I am very open to discuss it. We all have to decide what WE believe is right and wrong. All of us count. All of our individual points of view come in to play.

Our reaction to it all is what manufactures our reality as a whole, good or bad, yin or yang. We are all two dogs. We can all build on the positive or the negative. It's up to you as a human being what you are manifesting. We can all make a difference, you and I together. Let us make a better reality for us all to live in. We can DO THIS!

I truly believe that most humans believe as I do, that we should be tolerant of one another and nurture one another as we go.

We all deserve a do over. We all deserve to be able to recall the moves we make from time to time. However, fate is a cold mistress and she can be unforgiving, and all we can do is learn by hindsight and we aren't playing chess. Cold, but that is the way it is.

We learn from those stings of reality. We learn by the sacrifices of others, by osmosis. Sometimes from our own sacrifices, but we learn. This is the wheel rolling forever onward. We learn...and the wheel rolls on to the next one. All of us deserve another turn. We usually get it.

Sometimes we don't. The time is now to pay it forward so you got some karma coming your way. Give it willingly so the world will give it back with as much grace. We all need to gather together and recognize that we need one another.

We need to realize that our actions and words affect others. People will respect you or hate you, but it is up to you how you are perceived by others. When you are doing right that inner voice will change and at least YOU will recognize who you are.

We all need to share who we are a little more and put those I phones aside. There are real people on the other end of those face book pages. We need to get out of the house and get together in fellowship more.

A Tough Chapter to get down

Dying

You may find yourself in a position where no healing in the world is going to save you. I know this feeling and I won't get into all that because my own was a false alarm, but I had a few weeks to think about it all.

When this happens to you, and it will happen more and more with all the damage we are doing to one another and this world we all depend on, you have some choices to make, and some things to take care of.

First of all, you have to decide if you want to live or die. Plain and simple, there is no gray area at this point. This is a black and white question. Yay or nay, right now, what do you see for yourself in 6 months, or 4-5 yrs, 10?

Going to fight or die? We all have to own what you have done with the vessel we were given, and start to do some repair work on your own. If you have a family you owe it to them to do all you can to repair yourself and get on with it. We all have to pay our dues, and some of us pay it all, but you owe it to them to try.

You can do some powerful stuff by changing the acidity of your body.

Studies have shown that cancer cannot live in an alkaline body. Many things that you would think would be acidic like fruit and citrus actually break down to an alkaline base, as do most vegetables. Asparagus has a compound in it that corrects bad cell growth, do an internet search on what you can do proactively to help yourself. There is a ton of information at your fingertips.

Maybe they will offer you chemotherapy, and radiation treatment. There you have some choices to make. You will have to look deep into yourself to make these hard choices, and it helps if you have already given it some research and thought. Look into the medicine you are being given and I mean all of it.

ALWAYS do a web search or ask a pharmacist or whatever you have to do to get the information you need to take care of yourself, as many people see more than one doctor and get meds from multiple sources.

It is up to you to make sure they all do not work against one another. Make sure your doctor is keeping a list of everything you are taking. There is no central databank that your prescription information is programmed into and it is up to you to make sure. So ask your pharmacist, and fess up to all the other meds so you are well taken care of. Only you can take care of you.

Tell the doctor if you use illegal drugs, because they cannot help you if you are not honest with them. It is up to you to take care of you.

Even something as simple as grapefruit juice can drastically affect your health, as grapefruit juice interacts negatively with many common prescription drugs.

One of the things that struck me rather strongly when I had my poor diagnosis, was how they were giving me the runaround and all of them picking at my proverbial carcass as I thought for a while. I was amazed how much money had changed hands without my paying anything nor had I received any real healthcare.

They charged thousands and thousands of dollars for x-rays, MRI's, and for the 45 minute surgery they charged an astronomical amount of money. I was appalled by it all.

No wonder the cost of medical care is so out of whack. It's all a money game and our healthcare hangs in the balance. I have found it distinctly lacking just by common sense standards. Follow your own instincts. Listen to yourself.

There comes a time to talk to your family and come clean about it. This is best done in a straightforward and honest manner. I had time to realize I was dying, but I realized we all do, and that we can't pick the time or place. There is nothing we can do about it, and it happens to every single one of us. No one gets out of this game alive.

The thing is, I truly believe our soul or intelligence or cognizance, or something goes on. I didn't believe I was going to die, and I didn't know how to comfort my family that it was ok, that it is something we all have to deal with at some point in our lives and you never know when it is going to come up.

I had a chance to take part in a past life regression session with a good teacher. I honestly did not expect to be able to be hypnotized as I had tried a few times as a teen, and did not find a trance to be something I could achieve.

However after practicing daily meditation every night for a while now, I had much better focus and experience with deeply relaxed states, and it was a strange thing to experience. First I was just going with the guided hypnosis talk, and getting to a good and relaxed state.

At first I was just saying whatever came into my mind in response to the questions. Then suddenly very vivid scenes and memories started flooding into my mind and it was a lot of painful memories of things I don't care to relate here.

Anyhow I came away from there with a lot of food for thought and a whole new perspective on all of that past life stuff. It drastically changed my feelings on the permanent and final feel of death and it became a more transcendent thing for me rather than the final ending of my life.

After going through it a second time with the wife and simply sitting in on her session and meditating as she talked I had bizarre memories all too real of several different past lives coming in to my mind. Very interesting stuff is past life regression.

I no longer believe I am going to die. This vessel will pass on, but I will go on, and I am sure my wife will too. We have all had past life relationships and we will all have future life relationships in one form or another. The wheel of life and learning keeps turning, and as we approach the end of a cycle a lot is changing in our lives, and a lot of people are checking out of this reality.

Who could blame them, as this is getting to be a very hard world to live in.

When that time comes, try to be kind to your loved ones always. They love you and want to be near you. Be tolerant and enjoy every minute of it. This is what life is all about, soak up every second you can with your family and make the most of every minute.

Smile, even if it brings tears to your eyes, embrace those too. The pain is an experience all its own. If you try to take a look at it and pray to your higher self and go within, you can visualize the pain being warmed and healed, and you can breathe deep and you can get through it. Tomorrow will come no matter how bad it hurts and as surely as the rain.

Please always be gracious and thankful to your caregivers because if they did not love you then you would be someplace else going through this difficult time. These people love you, and you love them back. This is how you repay all their sacrifices when you need somebody.

Be that listening ear for a loved one's pain, even when your own pain is trying it's best to draw your attention. If you see someone that is in distress, then you be the person who says, "Hey, are you ok?" "What can I do for you?"

This will distract you from your own maladies and pull you away from the anxiety that dying causes you so inevitably no matter what your faith is.

The growth happens when you deal with adversity well and handle your business as best you can and still offer compassion to anyone you can. Give hugs and smile even when it brings tears to your eyes. You want to be remembered with a smile.

I guess I am lucky, as I have seen a few really sick people go out with total class all the way. It taught me a valuable lesson when I was faced with my own mortality, and I had role models to act on.

I had also seen the adverse of that and the negative vibes generated from all of that and I did not want to be that person remembered with someone spitting on the ground, but wanted to be the guy that people remembered with a smile. I want to go out like the people I was talking about above, with love, one way or another.

I know some won't remember me that way as I am two dogs, and that's just the way it is. I try to stay in the light but like every one of us I am a dark soul also. We all have our moments but we are all good and bad, and the mix changes from month to month and day to day. That is the human condition, and our reality.

When we are in terrible pain, the bad side may come out, and to those loved ones, please try to be patient with the ones that are passing, as they love you and they don't mean to be harsh, but they are in pain, and that can be some very heavy stuff to deal with when it gets bad. Please love us as we are you later in your life. The wheel comes around for all of us.

A lot of pain comes out as impatience or anger, and this is not meant to be so. The person hurting expects you to understand, and if you take on the responsibility of a dying person then you better get good with it, because this is the responsibility you are taking on and emotions can run deep in that ending time. Like that venison stew, this is life and it gets messy.

Anger and resentment is a part of death, every single one of us goes out scratching and clawing and mad as hell, especially if we are in pain. Respect that for what it is, a natural response to extreme pain and frustration and indignation at having to go out this way, no matter how it happens.

We are all full of emotion. All of us are needy, we all need to be accepted and loved regardless of the difficult people we seem to be. Some of the strangest people you ever met are some of the most interesting and have the most to tell you, if you ask the right questions.

Regardless of whether we are the dying or the ones caring for them, we all need one another and we will all need one another in our times of need, and believe me they will come. We will all have our moment of need and you better have somebody there to take care of you, so be kind to those around you as you never know who will step up and take care of you in the end.

How you go out, is up to you. Personally I hope I have the courage to smile right up to the very end and go out wishing everyone well and remembering dreams of a well loved life. That is how I would like to do it if I have a choice in the matter. How I will live up to that remains to be seen, but that is what I hope for in my life.

All my life I felt the need to be a better person. My Grandfather's on both sides were some very interesting people in their own right and instilled something in me that always made me know right from wrong.

My own father is practically a legend in his own time and is still a force to be reckoned with at 70 yrs old. I try to be a mix of my old school Father and my wife's Father, who is also old school with some Cherokee thrown in for an interesting mix. He has a peaceful soul but if stirred, a warrior resides within and one had better respect it.

I try my best to be peaceful as I go through life and offend nobody. This is not always possible if one speaks their mind as I tend to do. We all need to be our brother's keeper and step up when we see someone being abused.

This is what a man does if he wants to keep his own respect. Even as a man is dying, he needs to make choices himself as to how that will happen. A person can easily find a way out, or you can try to be strong as the vessel passes from you.

Try your best to take care of the details of passing ahead of time as that can get surprisingly expensive for those left behind. There are a lot of details that need to be wrapped up, especially if you are a homeowner.

Do you want the ownership of your home to be in question if you should suddenly pass away? Do you have a Last Will and Testament ready so that there is no misunderstanding of the aforementioned home ownership?

Get some Life insurance, at least enough to cover the burial of your own self and your loved ones. Decide if you want to spend that money for a burial ahead of time or if the much more economical option of cremation is for you. These choices need to be made beforehand.

Do you want a wake? An open casket funeral? All this stuff costs money is how I see it all like the doctors and the insurance payments from hand to hand, it is all a big money game.

When I am dead cremate me and spread my ashes around where I was the most happy. Let me be free and don't put me in any little box where I will be anchored to this world. Let me fly and blow like a leaf across the sky. It is not a bad thing, dying.

It is a metamorphosis like that wooly bear caterpillar crawling on the leaf. There is a spiritual creature locked inside that vessel of a body, and it will eventually bust out and fly free no matter who you are. It is inside of all of us, and we are a part of it all, every single one of us and the body has to die before it can fly free again. Somewhere inside you know this and yearn for it regardless of the pain it implies.

The All is waiting for us to return with the knowledge we have gained in this life.

Death is nothing to be afraid of. It is the living between now and then that is the thing to be considered. How you spend that time is very important to the good of us all. We all need to consider the people around us who are also going through a rough time right along with us.

If we could all live more in the now instead of the past and the future, you find you have much less to worry about than you thought you did. We have everything we need right this second. The world is not going to end today and more than likely we will wake up tomorrow and do it again. Everything is well right now.

The now is a much more comfortable place, as in this modern world, we seldom lack for the basics, like food, water and soap. We might be a little slight from time to time but we all make it work. We all cover those basics, and if you don't then I ask a blessing for you so that you may when you need them.

This writing did not always come natural to me over the last couple of years that this book came together. I battle with my own dark side just like everyone does and it was not that I was always in a positive place, but that is what I strived for. Life is hard as we go through it day to day and the yin and the yang both come into play. Writing this book came none the less. Some of the best stuff here was written in the depths of my soul when I was feeling my darkest.

Some people call this bi-polar. I tend to think we are all two dogs and all prone to the dark and the light. After all, you can't see one without the other, and I am very thankful that I have seen enough light in my life to know that anger and depression does not have to be the only thing there is to look forward to.

If you find yourself stuck in the dark, you know it. You know this is not the way that life should be. You can take steps to feel better and it may not be anything you find in this book. Something will resonate with you.

The thing is that you need to take an action, and do it with the intent of making everything better. Once you take one step, take another, also with the intent of making it better. We all need to live our lives with more intent in every action we take. Every positive action reinforces you as a positive force in the world.

This is like a ritual. It is like taking medicine. I saw studies done where thought and intent changes water crystals. If hateful thoughts are directed at water as it freezes the water freezes into a confused and not so attractive pattern, whereas when thoughts of love and peace are directed at the water it freezes into beautiful lacey structures that are beautiful to see. The difference is obvious and we as human beings are made up of mostly water. The point is our thoughts count.

You can see it in the ice crystals and it shows in you if you change your focus and make a habit of it. Look around you and take in this world, because it is not all bad. There is beauty in the small things all around you and all you have to do is open your eyes and take it in, and realize.

It can all look different if you can move your perspective a bit outside of yourself and quit listening to that lower self that whines and tells you that you are no good because of this, or because of that.

We ALL have something that we do that is not for the benefit of anyone else but is solely for us. Whether you drink, smoke, use drugs, got sexual issues, shop too much, or just pray a bit compulsively.

Maybe you just plain feel sorry for yourself, own yourself and get past it and realize that you can still be a productive and positive force in the world. Whatever you do you owe it to yourself. You deserve to do something for yourself even if it is not in everyone else's best interest.

The world is a painful place to live in and we all feel the sting of it from time to time. People tend to run from it in many different ways, but we all have to find ways to cope. I hope that something in this book resonates with you and helps you to cope with the difficult things in your life even if only a little easier.

Healing comes from within

If you find yourself broken, nobody can put you back together but yourself. You won't ever find any real happiness or peace of mind in a pill. It has to come from within you. It comes from changing that little voice in your head that is never satisfied with yourself, and you do that by doing those little things for yourself and others. Every time you do that little act, you are supporting and reinforcing your mindset changing as you have that one positive act behind you.

True peace can be had as the inside and the outside start to become one and the same and you start living up to the façade you present to the rest of the world as what you say and what you do get more in line with one another.

In a year you can have a real cumulative effect and change very much how you are perceived by people as you learn to smile more from the inside as well as the outside.

We all have something to contribute. None of us are so broken that we can't contribute something of ourselves. All of us could do something for somebody else and make their life a little better, and man that is a fact.

It is so hard to just cover the basics now. We all struggle so hard just to keep the roof over our heads. It is hard to imagine doing something to make someone else's life better. It doesn't take much, just take that action, with the positive intent to make it better, and it will, you just watch and see.

We all have this power. We all have something to offer even if it is just to help shovel your elderly neighbor's sidewalk. Try it. Kick it in and see if it doesn't make a difference in you and their lives. It WILL! Reach out and touch somebody! It will help you both, plain and simple.

We can all do this. We can all make it better for someone else, and when we do that we get better by osmosis. We have to take positive action with positive intent people. Pay it forward has never meant so much. We all owe it to ourselves and our loved ones.

At this time and this paramount moment, the entire world is envisioning some sort of apocalypse. I propose that we visualize love and peace and joy. If we all act together and meditate for a better world then that better world will come about despite the hardships that lie ahead.

We can change it all for the better and make it what we want it to be for us and our grandchildren. This world can be a better and more peaceful place if we all work at it just a little bit.

IF you take action to help someone else you will build relationships and friendships. These last a lifetime and are priceless as you go through your time in this world. We all need one another no matter how tough you think you are.

All we have is one another, and when the hard times come and they do for all of us, the ones you have loved may just be the ones to step up and take care of you.

Right now you may think you don't need anybody. You are wrong as you can be. We all need people around us to talk to and interact with. It helps us to grow. We all learn from one another. We are all teachers and we are all students in this world.

As I try to wrap this up and put into a form I can put out to you I want to reinforce how important it is to meditate with healing intent for yourself and those you love using the vital energy that flows through us all.

Remember there are energy points or chakras in your body that you can circulate that energy around in order to build and increase that energy, and that you can also scoop it up in your hands and apply it where you need it directly with your hands by simply visualizing doing so.

When you are visualizing this imagine if you will, gathering balls of liquid light in your hands and form it into a ball of energy as big as you like in front of you.

Visualize this energy as if it is a real and tangible force as it forms. Then project the thought of the perfect you into that ball of energy and imagine how it would feel to inhabit that perfect self.

SMACK your palms together and send that empowered visualization or prayer if you will out to the creator to put together for you. Your palms will be stinging to testify to the energy you just made, and coupled with the power of your creative thought it can be a very powerful tool once we get our very suggestible brains behind the process.

You can apply this to anything you wish to happen in your life. It all changes with a thought and that moment of realization when you suddenly know that you have made a change in yourself or someone else's life.

That is a pretty good thing to be able to experience, and if you just start putting a few of those good moments into your memory you will soon see that you are a better person and human being for just taking a minute here and there to help somebody else. It is self-reinforcement in its purest form.

It becomes a habit and before you know it other people will be looking up to you in a whole new way because they will have recognized that you are a good person. They might become a little better also just from seeing the example you are setting, and before you know it what comes around goes around takes on a whole new meaning.

Let's get it going around. Stir it up! I meditate to make my world a better place every single night for an hour or so before I fall asleep and now my brain does it whether I need the sleep or not. The time is always well spent and if I don't do it I don't sleep well anyhow.

I do this usually between 2 and 3 am (Pacific time) give or take. I know that if we all focus our thoughts together for a common goal we can achieve a huge improvement on the positive results accomplished in doing this.

It doesn't matter what time you do it and I realize I am up late compared to some, but wanted to put my time period down here so that the people that are up late at night tossing and turning as I tend to do will have a common time to meditate. Next time you find yourself tossing and turning and notice it is the early morning hours, put your intentions with mine and we will be stronger working together.

The power of our thoughts can change the world and it starts with making your thought process a better place to experience this world from. The world can look different from behind your eyes if you just let it happen.

Peace...

I am always willing to discuss anything in this book and can be contacted at Coopdog1911@gmail.com

Acknowledgements:

I would like to acknowledge my beautiful wife who has stood by me through the yin and the yang and been there with me for the last 30 years making my life better. She also made some very good suggestions in the editing of this book. She's an incredible human being. I love you Melissa. Thank you.

I would like to thank My Friends Bill and Hannah who started me on the healing path.

Many of the techniques in this book come from the writings and teachings of John Hill and his incredible "Change the paradigm" course. It changed my entire life. Thank you John.

A HUGE thank you to my daughter Mystery for creating the Two Dogs cover art for me and her endless patience helping with the formatting of it to get it just right for the cover.

Robert Bruce, "Energy work" and "Spiritual Self Defense"

Max Freedom Long, "The Secret Science Behind the Miracles"

Antonio Villoldo, "Shaman, Healer, Sage"

and many others incredible souls who have contributed to my own experience. Thank you as well.

About the author

I grew up in central Ohio. My wife and I married when we were young, and threw in together for this journey. I was raised in a non-spiritual household, where no talk was offered on the bible or God in general.

I first had to face the spiritual world when we were newlyweds and moved into a very actively haunted place. From there it just got more and more interesting and led me to the conclusions I ended up with in this writing.

Early on we moved out West to the Puget Sound area in Washington State where we continued to realize that all was not as we see it, and our spiritual life and training finally began in earnest. We continue to do healing and now I am a certifiable Kundalini madman, rocking my way through this life bursting with energy most of the time.

This writing was inspired by the many incredible things I experienced through the simple self exploration of meditating with positive intent. It is a gift you can give to yourself and doesn't cost you anything but a little time and you can raise the energy of everyone around you in the process.

It remains interesting...